Leading Groups in Corrections: Skills and Techniques

Ed Jacobs, Ph.D. and Nina Spadaro, Ed.D.

Mission

The American Correctional Association provides a professional organization for all individuals and groups, both public and private that share a common goal of improving the justice system.

American Correctional Association Staff

Printed in the United States of America by Graphic Communications Inc., Upper Marlboro, M.D..

ISBN: 1-56991-167-3

This publication may be ordered from:
American Correctional Association
4380 Forbes Boulevard
Lanham, Maryland 20706-4322
1-800-222-5646

For information on publications and videos available from ACA, contact our world-wide web home page at: http://www.aca.org

Cataloging-in-Publication data
Jacobs, Edward E. 1944-
Leading groups in corrections: skills and techniques/Ed Jacobs and Nina Spadaro.
p.cm.
Includes bibliographical references and index.
ISBN 1-56991-167-3
1. Corrections. 2. Group Psychotherapy. 3. Prisoners—Counseling of. I. Spadaro, Nina.
II. Title

HV9276.J33 2003
365'66—dc 21 2003043675

Dedications

To Wilson and Ross Harvey, thanks for teaching me so much.

— Ed

To my father, Louis M. Spadaro, with love to the first author I ever knew.

— Nina

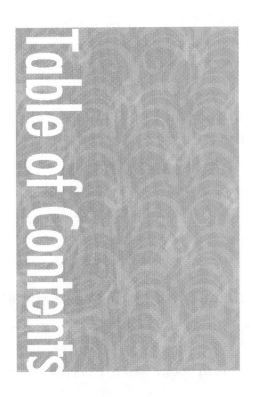

Table of Contents

Foreword

Corrections has always recognized the benefits of group counseling and programs for offenders as well as staff teamwork. And in times of tighter budgets, growing inmate populations, and larger caseloads, correctional professionals are using groups to maximize their services and apply their resources more efficiently. Almost all correctional employees—whether they are leading counseling sessions, conducting orientation, or delivering the day's announcements to staff—will find themselves addressing some type of group situation during their careers. While some people may be natural leaders, leading groups effectively demands skills that must be learned and practiced.

Leading Groups in Corrections: Skills and Techniques takes the reader through the basic concepts of becoming an effective group leader.

Written by two practitioners with more than forty years of combined experience, this book is ideal for those working in corrections and students in criminal justice and social work programs. The language is simple and direct, without complicated academic and clinical jargon. The authors, Drs. Jacobs and Spadaro, introduce important counseling theories with clear examples. Sharing their expertise, they have produced a practical guide to leadership in group settings.

The American Correctional Association (ACA) is proud to present another resource that helps fulfill its mission to improve corrections and enhance the professional development of corrections practitioners. I take great satisfaction in ACA's accomplishments, but I know that it could not achieve them without its members. If you are not a member of ACA and would like to share in our success, please join today by calling 1-800-ACA-JOIN.

James A. Gondles, Jr., CAE
Executive Director
American Correctional Association

Introduction to Group Counseling

The demands on correctional workers have never been greater due to the large caseloads and large numbers of individuals in jails, detention centers, and prisons. To deal with these demands, correctional workers are turning to group work as a way to handle more offenders in the same amount of time. Also, counselors are finding that group work can be effective in helping many who have come in contact with the correctional system. According to Silverman and Vega (1996) and Pollock (1998), most correctional treatment programs are group approaches.

The purpose of this book is to present information, skills, techniques, and exercises that can help you become more confident in your ability to lead groups in a correctional setting. This book is for those who are currently working in corrections and for those who are studying to work in corrections. Our intent is to make this a reader-friendly, relatively brief, introductory book with many examples of group sessions. This is a how-to book about group leading and not about counseling, theories, corrections, probation, or the criminal mind, although we touch on each of these subjects. Our emphasis is on skills and techniques. If you desire more in-depth reading on groups, you may want to read a comprehensive group counseling book by Corey (2000), Gladding (2003), or Jacobs, Masson, and Harvill (2002).

In this book, we use the term "correctional setting" to refer to any place that deals with persons who are there because they violated the law. Correctional settings include prisons, penitentiaries, jails, detention centers, residential centers, work camps, halfway houses, and probation and parole offices. In this book, we refer to all group leaders in a correctional setting as counselors, knowing that many may be correctional officers, social workers, psychologists, case managers, unit managers, house parents, or probation officers. Also, we refer to most of the members as offenders or inmates even though we realize that other terms may apply. For the most part, we use "leaders" and "they" to avoid the more awkward "he" or "she," but there are times when we use either "he" or "she" to refer to the leader.

Throughout the book, we provide many examples to give readers a sense of what happens in groups. The examples provide some idea of the many different skills that are needed to lead groups. We keep the examples rather brief and we present an excerpt from the session rather than presenting the entire session.

Why Conduct Groups in Correctional Settings?

There are a number of reasons for conducting groups in correctional settings. Groups are an efficient way to work with more than one person at a time. For instance, using a group format is more efficient when providing orientation information, drug information, or anger management training. Another reason for conducting groups is that many inmates need socialization skills and groups can provide this (Stojkovic and Lovell, 1997). Members learn from other members and inmates feel reassured when they hear others sharing similar fears and concerns (Masters, 1994). Also, inmates are often distrustful of the authority figures in the prison but may listen to their peers. Another reason to have offenders in groups rather than in individual counseling is that hesitant offenders end up talking more in groups as they hear fellow offenders share their experiences, thoughts, and feelings.

Pollock (1998) points out that groups can be quite helpful in that offenders are sometimes more effective than counselors at identifying game playing (*see* Elliot and Verdeyen, 2003). Too, offenders often are better than staff at confronting individuals who are attempting to delude themselves or others regarding treatment.

History of Group Counseling

The focus of this book is on group leadership skills and techniques. If you are interested in the history of group counseling, Gladding (2003) has an excellent chapter that discusses groups as far back as 1900. For a history of group counseling in corrections and research findings regarding group counseling, Rottman (1990), Smith and Berlin (1988), and Van Voorhis, Braswell, and Lester (2000) offer much information about groups that have been conducted in prison settings. They discuss the early drug treatment group experience, Synanon, and a probation program that became known as Daytop. Van Voorhis, et al. (2000) describe two adolescent programs, Guided Group Interaction (GGI) and Positive Peer Culture (PPC), that were popular from the1950s through the 1980s. Pollock (1998) offers a brief history of therapeutic communities and the rationale behind them.

Van Voorhis, et al. (2000) discuss research findings on groups in which Transactional Analysis, Rational Emotive Behavior Therapy, and Reality Therapy were used. One observation offered by Van Voorhis, et al. (2000) is that the reason many of the groups in the 1960s and 1970s were not successful may have been due to the passiveness of the leader. They stress the need for quality leadership and cite recent positive research on various treatment programs. Walsh (2001) also cites numerous programs that were successful with various offenders and inmates.

Types of Groups

Many correctional settings offer several different types of groups (Carp and Schade, 1992; Pollock, 1998; Walsh, 2001). Below we discuss four broad categories of groups: administrative, educational, treatment, and task groups. Within each of these categories are subgroups. Anyone who chooses a career in corrections will have the opportunity to lead most, if not all, of these types of groups.

Administrative Groups

A number of administrative groups are conducted in correctional settings. These groups are mainly for helping the institution run smoothly. Administrative groups include those that provide orientation, a town hall format, and crisis groups.

Orientation Groups. Many correctional settings have orientation groups for new inmates. These groups range from three to twenty-five members. Their purpose is to orient the inmates to their new setting and let them know the rules and procedures. Orientation groups are mainly for providing information, but the group format should allow for some positive interaction and discussion among the members.

Example: Orientation Group

It is twenty minutes into the session.

Leader: The purpose of this group is to help you get oriented to how things are run here. I've been talking about twenty minutes. I am going to let you share in small groups any thoughts or reactions. Also, this is a way for you to get to know each other a little bit. Let me get the four of you to group up and the four of you, and the five of you. Share anything you are thinking about what I have said or about being here. You will have about five minutes. (*Leader watches the group and sees that many are sharing. After about five minutes he stops them.*) Okay, are there any comments or questions?

Dorrie: Sally mentioned something about a time limit on the phone. What is the deal on the phone? Why can't we use it for as long as we want to?

Leader: That's a good question. Any other questions about the phone?

Sherry: Yeah, and what happens if you need the conversation to be private? Is there any way to make that happen?

Leader: Let me answer both of those questions pertaining to the use of phones. (*Leader answers.*)

Here, the leader got the members to talk in small groups, then asked for questions. One purpose of an orientation group is to get members more comfortable, and the small groups help to do that. Throughout the book, we offer many examples to provide a brief look at the actual behavior of the leader. Later in the book, we offer longer examples to highlight a technique or skill.

Town Hall Groups. Since a correctional setting is a small community, at times the entire prison or perhaps a housing unit or wing will meet in what is often referred to as a "town hall meeting." These meetings are usually meant to be an occasion when announcements are made and discussed and where prisoners can express their concerns on any issue pertaining to prison life. The leader has to make sure these meetings do not just turn into gripe sessions but rather are productive discussions about how things could run better in the prison (Johnson and Johnson, 2000).

Example: Town Hall Group

Leader: One of the main reasons for having this meeting is to discuss how we are going to deal with the bathroom situation, given the construction.

Jeff: It's going to make me late for work if I can't be in the bathroom at 7:00.

Ed: Hey, man, we all work! You're not special!

Leader: Hang on. Every work supervisor here knows that there are going to be problems, so things are not going to be as tight as usual. This doesn't mean you can be late all the time.

Roy: Can I change my job assignment? I hate it. I'll do anything else.

Leader: Roy, talk with your unit manager about that. Right now, we are talking about morning bathroom schedules.

In this example, the leader's role is to keep the members on topics that relate to everyone, which is why he did not focus on Roy's desire for a change in job assignments.

Crisis Groups. These groups meet only when there is a crisis at the facility, such as a riot, unrest in the prison, an escape, a fight, or a death. Each crisis group is different, but most of the time the leader needs to know how to calm inmates. The purpose of these groups is to inform and settle down the inmates. These groups can be very difficult to conduct when the crisis is a major one that has inmates upset.

Example: Crisis Group

Last week there was a big fight involving twelve men. They all are just getting out of segregation and the leader has them all in a room. Everyone is agitated.

Jim: I'm going to get your ass!
Bob: Stick it up yours, buddy!
Leader: (*With a calm, but strong voice*) Stop! Everyone listen. The fight is over. (*Softer voice*) I want all of you to either close your eyes or look down and breathe calmly. Actually, listen to yourself breathe for the next thirty seconds. (*Leader allows some time for this.*)
Mike: (*Angrily*) Where does Bob get off?
Leader: (*Interrupts with a calm voice*) Look, we've got to straighten this out since you all have to live together for a long time. We can spend a few minutes on what the problem is, but we are going to spend most of this hour on the solution.

In crisis groups, the leader often has to be very direct, which she was in this example.

Educational Groups

Many educational groups are conducted in prison to teach and process information. The counseling and interpersonal skills the group leader brings to the educational group will make a big difference. The leaders are usually the persons providing the information and then they lead discussions on the subject. In some educational groups that are for training purposes such as finding a job, members practice a skill and receive feedback from the leader and the members. In an educational group, the leader orchestrates the discussion so that much learning occurs. Here are some educational groups often found in correctional settings.

Prerelease Groups. They help prepare inmates for their release from one facility either to a halfway house or back into society. Subjects include teaching the legal and administrative procedures necessary for release, such as independent living skills, job-finding skills, money management, and the rules of probation/parole or supervised release.

Example: Prerelease Group

Leader: Today we are going to talk about job-finding skills. I want you to list five ideas for finding a job.

Gloria: I have a job when I get out.

Leader: That's fine but most don't. Gloria, list how you can find a job if something happens to the one you have. (*Leader gives them a couple of minutes to make their list.*)

Leader: (*Standing at flipchart*) Let's make a group list. Sandi, what did you put down?

The leader here gets input from the members, then teaches from the list that inmates have generated.

Drug groups. They provide information about types of drugs and their effects. These groups are often mandatory and may be a prerequisite for drug treatment groups (*see* Alexander and Pratsinak, 2002). Often institutions have purchased material that has information, lesson plans, and instructions for conducting drug education groups. Some of the material being used is current, interesting, lively, and presented in engaging ways and some is boring or irrelevant. If you are using purchased material, make sure it is useful material that is presented in a way that will keep members' attention. Sometimes leaders may need to modify it so that it fits their members' needs. (*see* Alexander and Pratsinak, 2002).

Example: Drug Group

Members have just finished watching a thirty-minute video.

Leader: What stood out to you about the film?

John: The part about the effects on the brain. That was scary.

Homer: I liked the part on different treatments. What treatment will we get in this group? I like drugs and see no reason to quit completely. I don't think I could ever quit using drugs.

Leader: This group is mostly educational. You will all be in treatment groups as well. I want to talk to you about the effects on the body. What do you remember about that?

Tom: I remember . . . .

The leader made sure to keep the group educational and not go into treatment issues.

Parenting Groups. One of the most painful aspects of being incarcerated is the loss of time with children (Crawford, 1988; Morton and

Williams, 1998). A valuable educational group in prisons is one on how to parent while in prison. One program described by Clement (1993) was the Virginia program, MILK (Mothers Inside Loving Kids). This program focuses on letter writing, calls, and visits, and teaches inmates how to celebrate special events. The group leader helps the inmates learn how to communicate through these different avenues. The group sessions give inmates a chance to express their feelings of loss and guilt. The sessions are helpful because members get a chance to see new opportunities to communicate with their children. The groups give members a sense of empowerment and hope.

Example: Parenting Group

Tina: My kids need me—they haven't even started school yet. I don't want someone else raising my kids.

Betty: I feel the same way. What am I supposed to do, drop out of their lives for three years and then drop back in on them when I get out? I can't see them because they are a thousand miles away.

Leader: Who said you can't raise them from here? There are plenty of things you can do to be a part of your children's lives.

Norma: Right! You're full of it.

Leader: No, I'm not. I have seen plenty of women be fine mothers to their kids from this prison.

The leader does a good job of letting the members know that she has much information and parenting-from-prison strategies.

Training for Jobs. In some prison groups, the leader teaches the inmates how to perform the jobs to which they have been assigned. Counselors usually do not lead these groups, but at times they may be asked to facilitate a job-training group.

Example: Job Training Group

Leader: Let me tell you some of the rules that apply to working in the kitchen.

Julio: Here we go again! More rules.

Leader: These are rules that apply to all food handlers all over the country. These are not prison rules. Some of you may go on to work in kitchens when you leave here.

Trevor: Why do I have to wear this stupid hat?

Leader: Anyone have an answer for that?

Andrew: No one wants hair in his food. I know I don't.

In this example, the leader focuses the members on a specific job requirement.

Treatment Groups

The purpose of a treatment group is to provide information, help, and support for inmates. Many treatment groups are therapy groups where individuals work on personal issues (Smith and Berlin, 1988). In some settings, treatment groups consist of helping members get along better with each other.

Drug Offenders Groups. Treatment groups for drug offenders are probably the most common groups run in prisons. In these groups, members get help with battling their addiction, guilt, shame, family-of-origin issues, and other personal issues that go hand in hand with their addiction. Members get a chance to learn about how addicts think and how they can change their own thinking. The focus is on overcoming denial, working a recovery program, learning relapse prevention skills, and other issues that arise. Leaders of these groups have to be knowledgeable about addictions and well versed in counseling theories. Much literature exists on drug treatment programs. Readers interested in leading these types of groups should acquaint themselves with some of the latest material on this topic. Verdeyen (1999) provides a discussion of drug abuse prevention programs in the Federal Bureau of Prisons. A search for drug treatment programs on the Internet can lead to valuable resources and information.

Example: Drug Treatment Group

This is in the fifth session of a therapy group.

Leader: Cheryl, do you want to say more about your guilt?

Cheryl: (*Crying*) Sometimes my guilt is so bad. I am not sure that even prison will help me get over what I did. (*Hangs her head*)

Shawna: Good Lord, this place is close to Hell as far as I am concerned. You are paying for what you did. You didn't mean to run over those people.

Patty: I know I am getting back with God and that is helping. Cheryl, are you praying for forgiveness?

Leader: Cheryl, where are you with religion—is that part of your belief system?

Cheryl: Oh yeah, but I know God is mad at me for what I did.

Leader: Say some more about God's feelings about you.

In this example, the leader holds the focus on Cheryl and gets her to focus on her guilt from a religious point of view since another member brought up the subject of God.

Sex Offenders Groups. Inmates incarcerated for sexual offenses often are involved in group therapy (Marshall, 1996; Walsh, 2001). Because the members are generally reluctant to attend, leaders of these groups have to be very skilled in group leading and well versed in the psychology of sex offenders.

Example: Sex Offenders Group

Leader: How do you think your victim feels about what you did?

Harvey: What do you mean?

Leader: (*In a kind, but firm voice*) Exactly what I asked. Your victims have emotional scars, some severe. Do you realize that?

David: I do now, but I did not at the time. I did some family counseling before I was sent here and it was rough. My daughter said all kinds of things to me. I have to tell you, I cried.

Marty: They won't let me see my daughters. That judge was out to get me. I've been thinking a lot about the judge. He . . .

Leader: Let's not get off track. Think about your victim.

The leader knows that one of the important aspects of a sex offenders group is to get the members to gain "victim empathy."

Gambling Offenders Groups. Inmates suffering from gambling problems need help if they are not going to repeat the problems that got them into trouble. Emphasis in these groups is on addictions in general and awareness of the issues and triggers related to gambling.

Example: Gambling Offenders Group

Leader: Any of you ever go to Gamblers Anonymous?

Serj: I did.

Leader: Was it helpful?

Serj: It was, but I quit going, and that's when I really got myself in the mess that led me to here.

Leader: Let's talk briefly about what all of you tried when you attempted to quit gambling and then we'll talk about what you can learn in this group.

Omar: Do you think it is wrong that I make my wife play the lottery each week?

Leader: Let me answer that quickly and then I want us all to talk about the different things you tried that didn't work.

This leader has a plan for the session and makes sure she does not get sidetracked by the members.

Anger Management Groups. Many incarcerated individuals have problems with anger. Sometimes the inability to control anger contributes to criminal behavior and problems within the prison. Prisons and jails often offer anger management groups to help inmates learn to control their anger (Cullen, 1992; Goldstein and Glick, 1987). Also, anger management is a component of most drug treatment programs. The more the leader has a theoretical understanding of anger and is able to teach that perspective to the members, the more beneficial the group will be. The better the leader's grasp of the theory of anger, the more this person will be able to teach that theory to the members and the more beneficial the group will be.

Example: Anger Management Group

Leader: I want to ask you this question about anger. The question is "Where does anger come from?"

Riley: People.

Darren: I don't know. All kinds of things.

Auggie: People and things.

Shane: Situations like your boss, traffic, being here in prison.

Leader: Any other ideas? (*No one speaks.*) What do you think of the idea "Anger is caused by what I tell myself, I cause my anger?" (*The leader writes these two sentences on the flipchart. The members stare at the two sentences.*)

Anger is caused by what I tell myself.
I cause my anger.

Riley: No way! My wife gets me mad all the time.

Leader: Are you willing to look further into that?

In this example, the leader has a definite theory (REBT—Rational Emotive Behavior Therapy) that he uses in discussing anger. He introduces it here and would use it throughout the rest of the sessions. (REBT is discussed in detail in Chapter 6.)

Stress Reduction Groups. In many institutions, stress is quite high for a number of inmates. By offering stress reduction groups, inmates can learn how to deal with the different stresses related to being in prison.

Example: Stress Reduction Group

It is twenty minutes into a stress reduction group and the leader is processing an exercise where she had the members list stressors in their lives.

Leader: Judy, what do you have on your list of stressors?

Judy: My court case, trying to do Christmas from this God-awful place, my roommate, worrying about my husband being faithful.

Leader: Someone else?

Vicki: I eat when I get stressed and I want to stop or I will gain too much weight.

Leader: We'll get to coping with stress a little later. In fact, I am going to go over some different ways to deal with stress as soon we hear everyone's list of stressors. For now, we are just sharing our lists. Do you want to share yours?

Vicki: Sure. I get stressed about all kinds of things. For one, my roommate is a pain in the ass.

The leader has gotten the members focused by using an exercise and tells the members that later they will discuss how they can cope with their stress.

Process Groups. Process groups are different from the other groups mentioned because they focus on the interactions of inmates in the group and in the institution. In halfway houses, these groups are conducted to help members relate better with each other. These groups focus on trust, better communication, anger control, being cooperative, being positive, and being able to work and play together. Knowing about group process and being able to draw out and cut off members are essential skills for these groups.

Example: Process Group

This is a meeting of ten female inmates who live together on a wing in a prison.

Leader: What would help people to get along better on the unit?

Sue: If some people weren't here.

Gloria: What's that supposed to mean?

Leader: Hold on. Look, there's ten of you here and you have to get along. No one is going anywhere.

Tanya: I don't like some of them and I never will.

Velma: That's because some of us are black.

Tanya: That's bull!

Leader: (*With a firm voice*) Stop. Calm down for a minute. In fact, I want you to take out your notebooks and I want you to write down three things that you think will make this group productive.

Therapy Groups. Many correctional settings have therapy groups for offenders who need to work on their personal issues. The issues can pertain to life in the prison, their street life, love relationships, relationships with family and friends, childhood issues, guilt, self-esteem, or any other issue about which the person wants to talk. Leaders of these groups have to be well versed in counseling theory and be skilled at involving members when one member is working on an issue (Corey, 2000).

Example: Therapy Group

Maddie: I have something I want to talk about. Last week was my birthday and I did not get even a card from my mother (*starts to cry*).

Joan: How old were you?

Maddie: Seventeen. I just hate my mother. She's the reason I am here anyway.

Leader: (*With a caring voice*) What do you mean?

Maddie: She was never home. She was always out drinking so I was left to myself and I hated it so I got in with this bunch of kids who were just out to have a good time. It was bad. I just kept getting in trouble. I knew I was heading for trouble. My life has been hell, and I have put my mom and grandparents through hell also.

Leader: Maddie, we can help you resolve this with your mom and your past. We can use one of those two models we talked about last week. In fact, let's talk about how all of you feel about your parents or whomever it was who raised you.

The leader is confident that she can help the members finish their "unfinished business" with their parents. She will use one of the counseling theories introduced in the previous session.

Family Counseling. Some counselors conduct family counseling sessions. These sessions can be seen as a group, and the skills discussed in this book are helpful to anyone doing family counseling. Correctional counselors need to be prepared to work with families, and the skilled leader can be quite helpful when there is tension between an inmate and her family (Van Voorhis, Braswell, and Lester, 2000).

Example: Family Counseling Group

Pam: Why don't you come visit more?

Husband: Because it's a long drive and Billy likes to spend time with his friends.

Pam: (*In an angry voice, turns to Billy*) So, your friends are more important than me!

Leader: Wait, Pam. I don't think that is what is being said. Your son is twelve years old.

Pam: What's age got to do with anything? He doesn't love me!

Leader: He is at the age where he really wants to hang out with his friends. Most kids his age would spend little time with their mothers.

Pam: But, I am stuck in this awful place!

Billy: That's not my fault! (*starts crying*)

Husband: Don't be so hard on the boy!

Pam: Don't take his side!

Leader: (*With calm voice*) Let me try to say what I think each of you is saying, and also, let's look at how each of you is really feeling.

In this example, the leader uses cut-off skills and summarization and tries to focus the session in a productive way. (These techniques will be discussed in a subsequent chapter.)

Task Groups

A task group meets to accomplish something such as planning how to handle an inmate, changing policies and procedures, or planning new programs (Hulse-Killacky, Killacky, and Donigian 2001). When led well, task groups are productive meetings where important things get accomplished. Unfortunately, sometimes task groups are boring and nonproductive because the leader does not have a clear purpose, does not focus the group, or lets one or two members dominate.

Example: An *Unproductive* Task Group

In this example, the group loses focus because the leader does not keep the members on task.

Leader: Today we have three people to staff: Brad, Scott, and Ross. We need to decide if they get to move up in levels and also in which treatment group to put them.

Karen: I like Brad. He's into NASCAR and I am a big NASCAR fan.

Felip: Are you really? I didn't realize that. Who do you root for?

Rose: Guys, come on, let's talk about Brad. Let me read you his psychological evaluation. It'll only take about five minutes or so. (*She* *reads while most people barely pay attention.*)

Leader: Questions about the evaluation?

Sandy: Did you use those new tests or the old ones?

Rose: I told everyone I was not going to use the new ones. The old ones get the job done and I am more comfortable with them.

Sandy: I like the new ones. How about others of you?

Sidney: I liked the new ones.

Example: A *Productive* Task Group

In this example, the leader keeps the group focused on the task of staffing the three men.

Leader: Today we have three people to staff: Brad, Scott, and Ross. We need to decide if they get to move up in levels and also in which treatment group to put them.

Karen: I like Brad. He's into NASCAR and I am a big NASCAR fan.

Felip: Are you really? I didn't realize that. Who is your favorite driver?

Leader: Let's talk about Brad. Rose has the psych evaluation. (*Rose acts like she's about to read the evaluation when the leader cuts in.*) Anyone need to hear it? I know I feel he is doing great and can move one or two levels. How do the others of you feel?

Rose: His evaluation is quite good.

Sandy: Did you use those new tests or the old ones?

Leader: Let's stay on Brad and then do the others so we can get out of here in thirty to forty-five minutes.

Concluding Comments

We hope this introduction has piqued your interest in learning more about groups and group leading. In the brief examples, we tried to provide a glimpse of the different types of groups and some of the things that leaders do when they are leading these groups. Throughout the rest of the book, our goal is to explain and show through examples the intricacies of groups and the art of skillful leading. The keys to being a successful group leader include the following:

- Having many group leadership skills
- Knowing how to use counseling theories in groups
- Knowing thoroughly the topics that you are covering in your groups
- Having the courage to try different techniques and intervention strategies

One way to greatly enhance your learning is to practice the skills that we are describing. If possible, you should lead a group while you are reading this book—it will make the material more meaningful.

Leadership Model and Characteristics

In this book, we present primarily an active, multisensory model of group leading although some groups may call for different styles of leadership. For treatment groups, we believe that the leader needs to be active and in charge. When leading a group of highly motivated members, as in staff meetings or task groups, a less active leadership style may be more appropriate.

An Active Model

In correctional settings, the leaders need to be active because usually when members are left in charge, nothing productive occurs. Our strong belief is ***people don't mind being led when they are led well***. Active means the leader does the planning, conducts the exercises, cuts off and draws out members, directs the focus, and does much of the therapeutic work using different counseling theories. Smith and Berlin (1988) advocate that the leader of offender and prison groups should be intensely involved with the group.

Group educators and trainers have varying opinions on how active a person should be when leading groups (Corey and Corey, 2002; Gladding, 2003). Some educators and trainers only teach the "facilitator" model where the leader is not very active (Yalom, 1995). The term "facilitator" is used instead of leader, to imply that the person in charge merely helps the members who are primarily responsible for the group and group process. Certainly, in some settings and even in a few groups in correctional settings, the facilitator model can be effective. However, we have found that the facilitator model usually does not work in correctional settings because group members have a wide range of needs, lack trust and commitment, and often have poor social skills.

According to Rottman (1990), research during the 1970s on groups in prisons found that overall they were not effective, but most likely this was due to the more passive model of leadership that was being used and the fact that untrained leaders were being used to conduct the groups. Braly (1976) and Kassebaum, Ward, and Wilner (1971) share reactions from former inmates. They report that former inmates and members of groups wrote about these groups as not having any leadership to prod inmates along toward areas of attention, and about how hours were spent in silence or complaining about correctional officers or other irrelevant matters.

Example: Active Leadership

This is in the middle of the first session of a group on anger for teenagers.

Bill: I hate it here!

Ted: So do I. I think we should contact our congressman.

Hector: That won't do any good. I tried it a year ago and got a form letter back.

Justin: It's impossible to not be angry, here at this place. I'm seventeen and locked in here!

Leader: (*With a calm but firm voice*) Look, guys. This is not a bitch session. We are here to work on anger in a constructive way. I want to try something. If you had to answer the question "Who or what causes your anger?" what would your answer be? After I get your answers, I am going to show you a model that addresses where anger comes from.

Example: Less Active Leadership

Bill: I hate it here!

Ted: So do I. I think we should contact our congressman.

Hector: That won't do any good. I tried it a year ago and got a form letter back.

Justin: It's impossible to not be angry, here at this place. I'm seventeen and locked in here!

Louie: Anger management—this is a joke. (*To the leader*) You can't help us with our anger!

Leader: How do others of you feel about that?

Bill: What can you teach us? Hell, in this place you better have a temper or people will get over on you!

Leader: Any others want to comment? Some of you seem angry now.

Bill: I want to talk about the guy who works the evening shift. He's an asshole.

In the first example, the leader sees that the session could quickly turn into a bitch session so he focuses the members' attention on something more productive. In the second example, he just lets the complaining continue. The active model where the leader directs the members will produce a group experience that will be more valuable than just letting the members vent.

A Flexible Model

Even though we advocate an active style of leadership, it is important to be flexible. The amount of leading during a session varies with the type of group and with the members. Group interest and participation can be stifled if the leader does not maintain an attitude of structured flexibility (Walsh, 2001). For instance, during the first few meetings of a task or treatment group, the leader may need to be quite active. As the group progresses, members may learn how to stay focused, so the leader would most likely become less active. One way to conceptualize leading is along a continuum that goes from the leader being very inactive or passive (1) to being very active (10).

1 2 3 4 5 6 7 8 9 10

Facilitator (passive)——————————Leader (very active)

In thinking about the continuum, most of the time a leader should be between a 5 and an 8, depending on the group's purpose and how well the members can stay focused without the help of the leader. Although we rarely believe leaders should go all the way to a 1 where they totally turn the group over to the members, there may be times when the leader leads at a 3 or 4 because the members are active, energetic, focused, and productive.

Most treatment groups need a leader at a 7 or 8 level to make sure productive work is accomplished. Referring to the first example in this chapter on the previous page, the active leader is at a 7 or 8 level, taking charge and making sure the session does not become a bitch session.

When a leader facilitates a treatment group at the 1 to 5 level on the continuum in a prison, the members tend to jump from topic to topic and person to person because most of the members try to avoid deep self-exploration.

In some task groups, the leader may be able to get the group started and then basically become almost another member, leading at a 2 or 3 level. In the example below, the leader makes sure the group stays on task, but does very little leading. This would be a 2 or 3 level of leading, which is appropriate because the members are focused.

Example: Appropriate, Facilitative Leadership in a Staff Work Group

Leader: What do you think we should do about the tension in the yard?

Jamie: I don't know, but we have to do something. A fight is going to happen real soon if we don't take some action.

Cyndee: I think we have too many out there at one time.

Carla: Only for an hour. We have to eat lunch. This schedule gives us a lunch and I for one don't want to give up my lunch.

Pam: Speaking of lunch, I thought they were supposed to open that staff dining room this month.

Carla: I heard.

Leader: (*Interrupts Carla*) Wait a minute. Let's get back to the tension in the yard. Our task is to come up with two ideas to give to the warden.

Shawna: I'm assigned to the yard a lot. I think we need to have inmates designated to certain areas.

Chris: That's a good idea but how could we enforce it?

Pam: We could be real tough the first few days and hope that it sets a tone. All I know is I agree with Jamie. We have to do something.

Leader: I agree. Can't hurt. We just have to come up with some new ideas. I know the warden expects us to come up with something.

Jamie: Let's think about what Shawna is saying—how to designate certain areas. I like that idea.

Carla: My uncle works at prison in Texas and he was telling me something they do to control the yard.

In this example, the leader steps out of the discussion after seeing that it is focused on the task.

Content and Process

All leaders have to understand the difference between content and process and how the two interact. In most groups, emphasis usually is placed more on either content or process, but this can shift (Gladding, 2003; Posthuma, 1999).

- "Content" refers to focusing on topics such as drugs, fears, guilt, fairness, or stress.
- "Process" refers to focusing on the interactions and feelings between members or between the members and the leader. Members not trusting each other or members being angry or hurt by other members or cliques within the group are all issues that pertain to the group process.

In education, orientation, or administrative groups, usually the focus is on the content, but even in these groups, issues such as members in conflict with the leader or other members can occur and then the leader may need to focus on the group process. Some treatment groups will focus on process—namely how people get along with each other in the group. Other treatment groups focus on content—members talk about their issues and the other members try to help. A leader has to pay attention to both content and process—know when to focus on content and when to focus on process. The purpose of the group sometimes determines whether the focus should be on either content or process, but often there is some emphasis on both. With experience, leaders learn to determine if the emphasis needs to be on process or content in order to be productive for most of the members

Example: Focusing on Content

The content topic is fear of losing one's wife.

Rijoul: I feel so afraid that my wife will find someone else while I am here.

Gus: Me too. Already she is writing less and visiting less. She says it's the drive that gets her. I think she wants to be home so she can meet someone.

Leader: Let's talk about this. This is a very common fear by the way. Do all of you have this worry? (*All but one member nods yes.*) Would it be helpful to talk about things you can do to keep your relationship going, even while in prison?

Example: Focusing on Process

Rijoul: I feel so afraid that my wife will find someone else while I am here.

Leader: Any one else feel that way? (*Silence*) This is a common feeling—no one else feels this way? (*Silence; with a serious, quiet voice*) There's something going on here. Anyone want to fill me in?

Gus: I am not saying anything. There are people here that wait for someone to say something and then they attack them.

Leader: Do all of you feel like Gus?

Tom: I do. I talked about missing my daughter a couple of weeks ago and felt like some were attacking me.

Dean: I don't feel people are always trying to be helpful.

Leader: Let's talk about these feelings. We want the group to be a place where you feel safe.

Jerome: I don't feel safe. There are some that only focus on others and not themselves.

Leader: This is definitely a problem so we need to talk about how to make this a safer place. I think we need to spend much of today's session talking about ways to make this group a safer place. Hopefully, Rijoul, we'll have time to come back to the issue which is bothering you.

A Multisensory Model

In correctional settings, group leaders who use a multisensory approach effect more personal change and have more impact than leaders who primarily use talking. Leaders have to use a variety of ways to generate interest and energy with inmates, and usually the more visual and active they make their groups, the more likely they are to be successful in reaching their members. Research shows that people learn in many different ways. Some learn visually, some through what they hear, and others through doing.

An effective leader will engage more members by using various multisensory techniques. Visual activities include such things as reading a short handout, showing movies, having members look at different lists or drawings on a flipchart, or having members look at a prop of some type, such as short and long fuses when talking about anger. Other good visual/experiential techniques are to have the members write, draw, or make something. Auditory techniques include listening to a speech, song, reading, or poem. Exercises that include getting up and moving around for a specific reason usually energize the members.

Multisensory techniques make groups more interesting and get more members involved. A multisensory approach gives leaders many more options than the standard "talk/listen" approach. Leaders who are creative and multisensory in their approach will almost always get more interaction and discussion than leaders who only provide information or control during a group session. Throughout this book, we offer many ideas on how to be multisensory and creative. If you want to read more about using a multisensory approach to counseling, *see* Gladding (1992), Jacobs (1994), or go to *www.impacttherapy.com*.

Example One: Use of "Fuse"

Members have been talking about anger. The leader decides to use the "fuse" technique to make the discussion more concrete.

Louie: I have always had a temper. Nothing I can do about it. My dad was worse than I am.

Leader: (*Takes out of a prop bag, four pieces of thick twine, all different lengths. One is about three-quarters of an inch, one about three inches, one about five inches, and one about twelve inches.*) I want all of you to look at these "fuses." Louie is saying that his anger fuse is like this one. (*Leader picks up a three-quarters-of-an-inch fuse*). I want you each to think how long your fuse is, and more importantly whether it can get longer.

Hector: I know I have got to get mine bigger or I won't last in this place.

Louie: How do I get a larger fuse? Mine's too short!

Leader: Anger management is about learning how to lengthen your fuse. Let me show you something.

Example Two: Use of Whiteboard (Blackboard or Flipchart)

Members have been complaining and the leader decides to make her point clearer by using the whiteboard.

Leader: I want you each to look up here at the board. What Diane is saying is "I can't stand it" (*Writes "I can't stand it" on the board. Members stare at the phrase.*) Most of you get yourself worked up by saying this to yourself.

Sherry: I feel that way all the time. I bet I say that twenty times a day here.

Connie: Well, it's true!

Leader: No, it's really not. The truth is, you all are standing it. Not liking it but standing it. Let's look at what you could tell yourself. (*Writes "I don't like it, but I can stand it." All stare at the board and seem deep in thought.*)

Not True	*True*
I can't stand it!	*I don't like it, but I can stand it*

Diane: Why do you have "I can't stand it" in the not-true column?

Connie: I was wondering that also.

Leader: Let's talk about it. (*While standing at the board*) Which one of these sentences really is true?

The leader makes the session interesting by using the whiteboard when teaching the theory of REBT—Rational Emotive Behavior Therapy —(discussed at length in Chapter 6.)

Example Three: Use of Chairs

Leader: Alex, let me show you something. All of you may want to think about this. (*Puts a chair about five feet in front of Alex*) In this chair is a guy who gets along with others here at the prison. Where you sit is a "tough Alex." Do you want to get to the other chair? Do you believe you can? (*Alex stares at the chair; other members are staring at the chair.*)

Wilson: I sure do. I want to get my ass out of here and I can knock off a year by getting along and staying out of trouble.

Alex: I am not sure if I can stay out of trouble.

Leader: Fine. But then, expect to be in trouble.

Sam: Alex, why do you want to make it hard on yourself? You can get to that other seat. No big deal. I was worse than you when I got here. Now, I've got all kinds of privileges.

In each of these examples, rather than just using words, a point was driven deeper through the use of a multisensory technique to which all members could relate.

Characteristics of an Effective Leader

To be an effective group leader, one must possess many positive characteristics (Gladding, 2003). One must be a good listener, have concern for others, and must be living a reasonably healthy and happy life. There are some additional characteristics that are needed to be a good group leader in a correctional setting, and even more are required of anyone leading treatment or therapy groups. Walsh (2001) offers an entire chapter on "The Self: The Principle Tool of the Correctional Helper." Below we briefly discuss some of the characteristics that Walsh and others describe.

General Characteristics of an Effective Group Leader

Comfortable leading others

Knowledgeable

Creative and courageous

Understands prison culture

Not frustrated by lack of apparent progress

Cares about people who are hard to care about

Firm yet not dictatorial

Characteristics of an Effective Treatment/Therapy Group Leader

Understands counseling theories

Has strong individual counseling skills

An Effective Group Leader Is Comfortable Leading Others

Leaders of groups should ask themselves this question: How comfortable am I around people and being seen as a leader among others? To be an effective group leader, you must be a people-person and be comfortable talking in groups. If this is not currently true for you, it is possible to change this by spending time with groups of people, making it a point to meet new people at every opportunity, and practicing talking in front of others. People who are shy or anxious around groups of people will not succeed at leading. Oftentimes, those who are uncomfortable around people do not like to stand out in a group, and they also do not like being in charge. The corrections population requires a firm, understanding person who is comfortable being in charge.

An Effective Group Leader Is Knowledgeable

Each group has a topic or subject. Effective leaders must be knowledgeable about the topics that are brought up in the session or are likely to be brought up in the session. This may seem obvious, but we frequently hear of groups being led by leaders who know little or nothing about the topic. Those who need more knowledge about different topics can find an abundance of information in books, on tapes, on television, or on the Internet. Also, there are numerous local, state, and national workshops that individuals can attend on many of the subjects that arise in groups.

An Effective Group Leader Is Creative and Courageous

Good leading takes courage. Many times leading a group requires a unique or creative action. Skilled leaders have the courage to do what it takes to make groups more effective. The courageous group leader is willing to confront a member in the group, challenge a member who is trying to take over the group, push a member to the point where she breaks through her denial, or screen out a member who is being totally disruptive. Smith and Berlin (1988) in their section on criticism of group counseling state that leaders should be courageous enough to take risks both in use of techniques and in the introduction of subject matter.

Often leaders will need to do something dramatic during a session to get the attention of the members. It is necessary at times to step "outside the box;" yet, many correctional workers are reluctant to do so. Leaders who have the courage to be creative will be more effective since the inmates are going to need to be nudged, pushed, challenged, and entertained. It is the responsibility of the group leader to have the courage to try all angles to help inmates grow to their potential. Throughout this book, we give many examples of being creative, courageous, and thinking and acting "outside the box."

Example: Doing Something Creative and Courageous

The leader knows she needs to do something that will get the members' attention and even put them on the spot. During a task group of eight staff members, the leader sees that tension is building because people are arguing about holiday coverage. People are angry. The leader knows there is a large conference table down the hall.

> **Leader:** *(With a firm voice)* Stop! I want all of us to get up. We are going to all walk down the hall and take a chair around the conference table which I am now going to label the "peace table." Don't pull your seat up to the table. (*People get up and walk down the hall and take a seat. The leader writes on a large piece of paper PEACE TABLE and puts it in the center of the table.*) Only come to the table if you are ready to negotiate. No one is going to get exactly what he or she wants. (*Some at first are hesitant, then slowly move their chairs to the table. Three hold out. The leader starts the discussion with only those at the table. Eventually, all come to the table.*)

An Effective Group Leader Understands Prison Culture

For correctional workers in a prison, an effective leader needs to understand that the prison community is a world unto itself, with a clear pecking order and rules of etiquette (Silverman and Vega, 1996). Walsh (2001) describes how the prison subculture works and why it is so important that the leader should understand this. For example, when one of the authors was leading a group in a drug unit, she understood that "Doc," an older inmate in the unit, was respected by the inmates in her group, so she was careful to refer to him in a respectful manner. She also knew to knock on the door to make her presence known before entering the group room if a conversation had already begun among the members.

Inmates often are hypersensitive to any indication of what they might term "disrespect." Leaders need to be aware of the culture and language of the correctional setting and use this knowledge to make themselves more approachable and effective. Also, understanding the culture helps leaders to avoid offending the inmates.

A Skilled Group Leader Is Not Frustrated by a Lack of Apparent Progress

Since people in the correctional system are not there for personal growth, progress is often slow. All correctional group leaders have to be prepared for little or no noticeable change. If you are a person who needs to see quick results, working with the prison population probably is not for you. Often, what you are doing is "planting seeds," so patience and high tolerance for frustration are essential with this population. For those who are inexperienced, talking with experienced correctional workers can be inspiring because they have stories about how long it took to see change in certain inmates and how those inmates went on to be model citizens in and out of the prison. Experienced leaders maintain their optimism by remembering that true change takes time and progress is often slow with this population.

A Good Group Leader Cares about People Who Are Hard to Care About

It is not easy working with the prison population. Postman (1998) states that inmates may be less "likeable" than other populations and they may vent their frustrations and anger at the counselor (*see also* Welo, 2001). Some of the people you will encounter are difficult to like because they lie and are rude, pushy, mean, uncooperative, and ungrateful. Also the inmates try to "con" you (*see* Cornelius, 2001; Elliot and Verdeyen, 2003). Prettyman (1981) describes how offenders "con" the inexperienced leader by learning what is expected and go through the process of "being cured." The skilled correctional worker realizes that underneath all this is a hurting human being who can learn how to live life in a better way. Those working in corrections have to have thick skins because the offenders will test them in a variety of ways, especially if the person is leading them in a therapy group where she is trying to help them to change. The skilled leader sees it as a challenge to try to reach difficult offenders and is not thrown off by any attacks or "cons."

A Strong Group Leader Is Firm yet Not Dictatorial

As we said earlier, correctional groups with offenders need strong leadership. However, if the leader acts like a dictator, the members usually will rebel either by attacking verbally or by withdrawing. It is important to distinguish true strength from weakness masquerading as strength. Use of status, intimidation, and subtle or not-so-subtle threats are not effective in building a good group atmosphere. Walsh (2001) offers an excellent personal story about how he "puffed up his sense of importance when dealing with a medical doctor who was in his group." As he said, this was a very poor way of handling the situation. The key is to be firm but not dictatorial.

An Effective Therapy Group Leader Understands Counseling Theories

Counseling theories explain why people behave the way they do and what they need to do to change. Knowledge of one or more theories is absolutely essential for leading treatment groups (Van Voorhis, Braswell, and Lester, 2000; Walsh, 2001). Unfortunately, lack of knowledge about theories is one of the major downfalls of therapy groups in correctional settings. In Chapter 6, we discuss three theories and how they can be used effectively in correctional groups.

A Skilled Treatment Group Leader Has Strong Individual Counseling Skills

To be an effective treatment group leader, one must have strong individual counseling skills because problems will be presented and the members will have no idea of how to help. The leader's responsibility is to direct the helping, and often leaders will find themselves conducting counseling while the other members are mainly watching. Therefore, the more skills the leaders have, the more impact they will have. One of the best things leaders can do to increase their effectiveness in leading treatment groups is to get as much supervised individual counseling experience as possible. Our belief is that if individuals do not have a thorough knowledge of at least one counseling theory and strong individual counseling skills they should not be leading treatment or therapy groups.

Concluding Comments

The style of group leading depends on the type of group and its members. Leadership style flows along a continuum from being very facilitative to being very active. Using an active multisensory, theory-driven model for most groups will make leaders more effective. To be effective, leaders also will need to be comfortable leading others and be knowledgeable about groups and the subcultures of those with whom they are working. They will need to be well informed about the subjects they are discussing with their members and not be easily frustrated by the seeming lack of progress on the part of the inmates. For treatment groups, leaders will need to be experienced with individual counseling, knowledgeable about counseling theories, and have knowledge about working with offenders.

Challenges in Conducting Groups in Correctional Settings

According to Walsh (2001), institutional counseling is the ultimate challenge for the criminal justice helper. A goal for this book is to excite you about the rewarding possibilities of doing group work as a correctional worker so that you are not discouraged when confronted with the various challenges and frustrations inherent in the field of corrections. A number of unique problems exist in correctional settings, and correctional workers need to be familiar with them. These can be divided into three categories: the population, the setting, and the policies. Being aware of these potential areas of trouble will help leaders in both their preparation for working in this field and in their actual day-to-day work in the field.

Population

Nonvoluntary Membership

In one sense, all the groups of incarcerated individuals are nonvoluntary; inmates did not consciously choose to be living in a prison. Within the prison population, some members will want to be in a group. Unfortunately, many of those who choose to be in groups in a prison setting do so because it looks good for advancement or for a reward of time off their sentences in the prison system. Many also sign up to be in a group because they see it as a way to pass some time. However, many groups are mandatory so the leader has to deal with those who are angry about having to be in a group. Only a small percentage of each group's members are intrinsically motivated. Obviously, leading groups with nonvoluntary members is much harder than leading groups with those who are coming because they want to learn about ways to live more effectively.

Because of the generally nonvoluntary nature of groups in correctional settings, the demand for the leader to be able to sell or "market" the group is much higher than in most counseling settings. Corey (2000) comments that the key to successful participation lies in thorough member orientation and preparation and in the leader's belief that the group process offers something helpful to inmates. The leader has to convince the members that the group can be useful for them in many aspects of their lives. Many group leaders fail to realize that a major part of group leading is marketing. Too many leaders mistakenly get right into the content or subject matter without focusing on getting the members interested and eager to learn and change. Marketing is very important in the first few sessions and needs to be continued to some extent in almost all of the sessions because the members are nonvoluntary.

New leaders come with great enthusiasm only to be frustrated by the lack of interest and commitment on the part of the members. If leaders plan for this ahead of time, their frustration level should be minimal. They should anticipate working with nonvolunteers. Their challenge is to lead such interesting and helpful groups that the nonvoluntary members actually start to look forward to coming to their groups. The best way to do this is for the leaders to be knowledgeable, passionate, positive, and to show that they believe the group can be a very valuable experience.

Screening

The freedom to screen potential group members will vary. In many correctional situations, leaders are allowed to screen the members. Screening is the process of selecting and sorting members for specific groups based on interviews or information gathered from inmates' files or from other staff members. Screening is an important factor that when overlooked can be detrimental to the effectiveness of a group program. The benefit of screening is that the leader can select members who seem to be interested and appropriate for a given group, such as one on anger management or improving communications. Some correctional settings allow leaders to screen out potential members based on their lack of interest, their negative attitude, or their lack of readiness to be with others who are sharing at a personal level.

In some correctional settings, offenders are mandated to be in a group. In these settings, the purpose of screening is less for selection and more about sorting members into various groups according to their abilities, attitudes, or interests. Leaders try to place members who will work well together or who will not be hostile toward one another. Also, the leaders have to decide where to place the very negative members and whether to put them all in one group or to mix them with members who are interested and want to gain something from the group experience. Usually it is best to put a negative member with positive members in hopes that the negative member will learn from the positive ones. At times, however, leaders may want to group negative members and then try some creative things to see if they can turn around the members' negative attitudes.

An important benefit of screening is grouping members who are compatible with one another. In many situations, certain offenders probably should not be in the same group because they despise each other or one is very hostile toward another. Some of these attitudes are personal, some cultural, and some gang-related. There are strong prejudices in prison populations and some individuals are not interested in overcoming those prejudices. On the other hand, there may be times when leaders will want to tackle the different prejudices by putting members in groups where they know there is discord. Racial and sexual-orientation prejudices should be considered when selecting members for groups. We are not saying to avoid putting people in groups who have these prejudices, but rather that placement of members should be based on the purpose of the group and the skill of the leader. Groups can be an excellent place for inmates to work on prejudices, but the leader must be able to handle the potential trouble.

Leaders can screen for group members in three main ways: direct interview, paper review, and staff recommendation. Interviewing perspective members is probably the best way to screen and usually is possible since the potential members are living on site or are people on your caseload. If the leader does an interview, she will want to have some specific questions about why they want to be in the group, what their thoughts are about the subject or purpose of the group, and any concerns they may have about other possible members. It would be important to know if there are some people they absolutely would not want to be with in a group.

In lieu of an interview, often leaders can gather much information by looking in potential members' "jacket" or file. If a person has been through the court system, the leader usually can get helpful social/psychological data to get an idea of what groups might be appropriate.

A third way to screen is to get recommendations about who needs a group or who would be good in a group from caseworkers, correctional officers, unit managers, or other workers who know the inmates. It is still a good idea, if possible, to talk with these potential members. Also, it is a good idea, if possible, to use the first meeting for screening, meaning that not all who come to the first group will necessarily be in the group (Corey, 2000). Selective screening can help eliminate many problems in groups but unfortunately, in many settings, members will just be assigned to the group because it fits their schedule.

Selective screening is not done only at the beginning. In most institutions, leaders will be able to screen out members if they are acting inappropriately. Many strategies should be tried before leaders decide to screen someone out of a group. They can do the following things:

- Talk with the member outside of the group
- Have other members talk with the member outside of the group
- Have the members give the person feedback during a session
- Limit the person's talking to one or two times a session
- Invite the person to come but have the member be completely quiet for a session or two

If none of these strategies work, the leader, most likely in private, should tell the person he or she no longer can be in the group. When screening out a member, the leader will want to discuss it with various staff members to see if it is the best idea and to let them know of the decision and when it will occur—just in case there will be some reaction on the part of the member. Screening a member out is sometimes difficult but it is the leader's responsibility not to allow a disruptive member to dominate and ruin the group experience for the other members who could benefit from the experience if the one disruptive member were told not to return to the group.

It is important to realize that some institutions demand that all offenders be in a group. Also, in some settings or situations, leaders do not get to screen out members because members are there for orientation, prerelease, or a town hall group. This makes the leading more difficult. Throughout this book, we offer many tips for handling situations dealing with inappropriate members.

Commitment

When leading a group of offenders, the leader will want to assess members' commitment to being in the group. Naturally, voluntary groups are usually easier to lead because the members want to be there. Lack of commitment to the group experience is a major problem in prison groups since the members usually have only a vague understanding of what it is they are signing up for or being forced to be a part of. In most other counseling settings, members make a conscious decision to be in the group. In correctional groups, this is not the case. So, one of the first tasks of the leader is to get the individuals committed to trying to be contributing members. One important thing to find out is their view of groups. Some have a negative view of groups based on what they have seen on television or in movies. Others have had bad experiences in groups, so their commitment is quite low. On the other hand, members who have had a good previous group experience often can be used to help others by having them tell how they have benefited in the past from being in groups.

Below are two examples of what may happen when members are not committed.

First Example: Noncommitted Members

This is sometime during the first session of an anger management group.

Leader: What would you like to get from this?

Don: When is this over? This is bunch of bull. I got better things to do!

Leader: How about others of you? Surely some of you have something to say about anger (*silence from all members*).

Second Example: Noncommitted Members

This is during the second session of a treatment group dealing with drugs.

Leader: Any thoughts since last week?

Hero: About what? The food here sure is bad. They've got to give us more choices.

Leader: I want comments or thoughts about drugs and what we talked about last time regarding what drugs have done to your life.

Tony: Can I get a drug to help me sleep?

Leader: Seriously, anyone think about what we discussed?

José: All I can say is I can't wait to get high (*Everyone laughs*).

These examples show that leaders of groups will need much skill and creativity to engage some inmates. Staff members or supervisors may tell you that it is not possible to get most members committed to the group experience. We disagree. We believe that it is possible to increase the commitment level of many, if not all, of the members of groups. The best way to do this is to make the group interesting, relevant, and helpful. No doubt it is hard to get some offenders committed to changing some things about themselves, but we are writing this book because we believe that many valuable groups can and should be led in correctional settings. Those who complain about the inmates' lack of commitment often are leaders who need better counseling skills, better group leadership skills, or new and different exercises to use in their groups. Also, those who complain may need to learn to be more creative, courageous, and motivated.

Trust

Leaders always must pay attention to trust levels when leading groups in correctional settings. Lack of trust is a major problem. Unfortunately, many inmates in jails or prisons either have been hurt by others or they have hurt others. Members do not trust each other, and they do not trust group leaders because they see the leaders as part of the "system." This creates major problems for leaders because groups cannot be productive if the members do not trust the leader or other members. Members certainly will not share very deeply if they think the other members or the leader cannot be trusted.

A leader must understand trust and distrust in prison settings. Factors leading to mistrust include the following:

- The mental health of the members
- The lack of comfort with being in custody
- The tone and the level of tension of the correctional setting itself

Lack of Trust Due to the Mental Health of the Inmates

Some in correctional settings have had positive past experiences with others and have the ability to develop a moderate-to-high level of trust if given the opportunity. Unfortunately, these types of inmates are in the minority. Most inmates have difficulty with trust. Also, group leaders need to be prepared to deal with inmates who are either acutely mentally ill or have a chronic personality disorder which interferes with their ability to trust. Some members in groups have antisocial or paranoid personality disorders (Pollock, 1998; Samenow, 1984). Needless to say, this makes trust building much more of a difficult task. The scenario below illustrates what leaders could face with inmates who are not mentally healthy.

Example: Suspiciousness of Members

Leader: I want to talk about your ability to share your thoughts and feelings with others.

Ted: I am not sharing. You'll tell. You'll tell the judge. I need a wife to share with. Can I leave? I want to leave.

Leader: (*Knowing that Ted sometimes can become quite disturbed*) Ted, you can sit quietly but you do have to be here for this hour.

Bill: Ted, you're sick! A wacko!

Leader: Bill, remember, we're not here to attack others. As for the topic of sharing, I am not so interested in you sharing in here, but rather, I want you to think about whom you do share with.

In this example, the leader knows he has members who are going to be difficult, so he is ready to cut off quickly, as he did in this excerpt. The leader knows that it is going to be difficult to get much trust in the group, so he is going to focus more on the topic of sharing outside of the group in hopes that some will share in the group. The leader plans to teach some ways to help members improve their ability to share since she knows that the members have poor styles of communication and trust almost no one.

Lack of Trust Due to Comfort Level with Being in Custody

Trust in correctional groups is sometimes affected by how comfortable the members are being in custody. Almost no one likes being imprisioned, but some adapt much more easily than others. Leaders should be especially alert to inmates who are new to a facility or who are waiting for a trial, sentencing, or transfer. Inmates who are waiting for sentencing or transfer are often "freaked out" by being in a prison, or they believe that everyone around them is evaluating them or out to get them. When leading groups with people new to jail or prison, the leader should pay attention to their level of comfort. The more uncomfortable they are, the harder it will be for them to trust in a group situation.

Lack of Trust Due to Level of Tension in the Correctional Setting

Correctional settings have more tension than most noncorrectional settings and lower-security facilities have less interpersonal tension than higher-security facilities. Leaders always should be aware of the level of tension where they are working since it is a factor that influences the amount of trust that they can expect in a group. When leaders are planning a group, they need to decide what they can do to reduce the tension or if they need to adjust the group plan. Many times when the level of tension is high, the trust level will be low. When this happens, the leader must make adjustments in the purpose, focus, and activities.

Throughout this book, we refer to trust issues and how to deal with them, since much of the burden of creating a trusting environment falls to the leader because the members usually lack skill in trust building. In Chapter 8 we discuss trust-building activities.

Setting

Some correctional settings have group rooms or good meeting places but often groups in jails and prisons meet in less-than-ideal settings. Some meet in very bad situations. Meetings are held in rooms where others may be watching television, recreating, eating, or where a snack machine is located. In many situations, there is no privacy and inmates or staff might be listening or observing. In some cases, it is policy to have a correctional officer present. Leaders and potential leaders should be prepared for group meetings to take place in locations that detract from the experience. Naturally, leaders should try to do what they can to improve the setting. We have found that skilled leaders are usually able to overcome even the worst settings by anticipating the distractions and engaging in activities that keep the members interested and involved.

Policies

Van Voorhis, Braswell, and Lester (2000) explain that offender counseling and treatment often becomes frustrating because of the amount of paperwork and constraints placed on the counselors or probation officers. Faith (1993) and Walsh (2001) also write about the frustration and problems associated with counseling in the field of corrections.

Corey (2000) states that "a common problem among those who regularly do group work in an institutional setting is the constant struggle to retain dignity and integrity in a system where the administrators are primarily concerned with custodial care or with putting out 'crisis fires' and are relatively indifferent to the pursuit of genuine group therapy or counseling" (p. 37). The key is for group leaders to focus more on their groups and not the policies, except when there is a chance that the leader can get the policies changed. These problems do exist, and it is up to the group leaders to deal with them and to work within the system while, at the same time, maintaining their professional standards and integrity.

Size

The ideal size for groups depends on the type of group and its purpose. Orientation groups and town meetings can be large without compromising the purpose of the group. Also, educational groups can have as many as ten to fifteen members and still be successful. Many of the skills in this book can be helpful for groups larger than that, but any educational group with more than fifteen members is more like a class and not really a group. Task groups can work well with as few as four members and as many as eight-to-ten members. For treatment groups, the ideal size is six-to-eight, although many times leaders will not have the luxury of having this ideal size. In settings such as jails, there may be only three or four members, but in prisons, often groups end up being twenty-five or more due to the policy of the institution. Leaders of treatment groups of more than twelve have to be exceptionally skilled to make the groups reasonably successful.

When groups are quite large, it is impossible to always hear from every member. Activities that require members to share in small groups of three or four are helpful in that members get a chance to talk—just not in front of everyone. Also activities where the members can benefit from watching or listening are excellent for large groups. Written activities can be helpful in large groups because everyone can feel involved as they work on answering some questions or completing a rating form or sentence-completion activity. Number, word, or phrase rounds can be very helpful in large groups. (A round is an activity where everyone speaks. Rounds are described in detail in Chapter 7).

Treatment groups of twenty members rarely can get to any level of depth if the leader tries to hear from each member. The leader should regularly encourage all the members to think and apply what is being said to their own lives, but the leader cannot hear from everyone all the time and expect to have time to take the group to any meaningful level. Ideally, the members get engaged and involved by listening and watching as some members work on their issues.

For large treatment groups, (twelve-to-twenty), the fishbowl technique is helpful. This technique involves having an inner circle and an outer circle. The inner circle is made up of six-to-eight members who are interested in working that day on the specific issues being discussed, or perhaps membership in the inner circle is done on a rotating basis. The outer circle is composed of the other members who are observers but not part of the working, inner circle. That is, they listen to all that is going on, but the leader is mainly focusing on those in the inner circle. If someone in the outer circle feels compelled to talk and wants to work on her issue, she can join the inner circle. By using this technique, the leader can focus on a few of the members who want to work and the leader does not have to attend to all of the group's members. When using the fishbowl technique, leaders have found that many of those in the outer circle benefit from just listening and watching.

Mandatory Participation

One problem that exists in correctional settings is mandatory group participation. Most of the time, even if the groups are mandatory, the skilled leader can get members to become interested and involved. At times, mandatory membership may result in members being very disruptive because they do not want to be a part of any type of group experience. Most institutions have a disciplinary policy, which makes it possible to remove members from a group if they are consistently being disruptive, but in some situations the group leader will have to deal with those who have to be in the group but absolutely hate the experience.

For these negative, hostile members who are in a group of six or more, the fishbowl technique can be helpful in that those members can be assigned to the outer circle where they cannot disrupt. This meets the requirement of having the members in a group, but they are not in a position to sabotage the experience for the other members. We have seen situations where these members actually get interested and make the choice to participate after sitting in the outer circle for a few sessions.

Revolving Membership

A special problem that exists with correctional groups is that institutions get new inmates daily and these new inmates are put immediately into groups, potentially disrupting the comfort and trust of the group. Any worker in corrections has to be prepared for groups that have members coming and going on a regular basis. In later chapters, we discuss how to introduce a new member, how to say good-bye to members leaving, how to help members adjust to a new member, and how to help the new member phase into an established group. Skilled leaders learn to deal with these problems fairly easily. The unskilled leader focuses too much time and attention on those coming and going, which can cause the other members to lose interest because they feel the group is not being valuable to them.

Concluding Comments

This chapter focuses on typical problems within the correctional setting. A major problem is that most prisoners are not committed to groups in which they are placed. Also, tremendous trust problems exist due to the inmates' level of mental health, comfort, and the tension within the institution. Often leaders are asked to conduct groups in far less-than-ideal conditions. Sometimes, institutional polices may create major concerns for group leaders, such as policies that call for large groups and for all inmates to be in groups. If an institution has policies that are detrimental to a successful group program, the leader can try to change these policies; but all group leaders must be prepared for policies and procedures that are obstacles to running successful groups.

Workers in correctional settings who are prepared for these problems usually can figure out methods to make groups productive. Having excellent group skills is one of the best ways to overcome these disruptive factors. We present the challenges not to discourage you but rather to encourage and empower you. Anticipating these problems will help you to deal with them effectively.

[illegible]

Common Mistakes in Correctional Group Leading

Group leading can be satisfying if the leader can avoid some of the common mistakes that can cause the experience of leading groups to be unrewarding (Kottler, 1994). Leaders who avoid these errors not only conduct better groups but they find leading groups to be challenging and gratifying. Leaders who continue to make these mistakes often find group leading to be unfulfilling and stressful. In this chapter, we discuss nine mistakes that are common among leaders who work in various correctional settings:

- Allowing inexperienced or unskilled leaders to lead groups
- Not planning
- Not making the group meaningful—just filling up time
- Being intimidated—giving in to the negative members
- Not interrupting members
- Spotlighting members when trying to draw them out
- Responding to every comment
- Not having a theory
- Not involving other members when working with one member

Allowing Inexperienced or Unskilled Leaders to Lead Groups

Often correctional officers or other personnel are required to lead groups when they have no experience. We strongly suggest that readers who find themselves in this situation request some training so that they are at least minimally prepared. Reading this book is one step that should help those interested in being successful group leaders. Supervisors and potential supervisors should make sure that they do not ask inexperienced or untrained people to be group leaders. Unfortunately, the use of unqualified leaders has been common in correctional settings and has resulted in unproductive groups and treatment programs. Research in the 1970s pointed to unqualified leaders as a major reason why group programs were not successful. Now, group leaders are being better trained and new research is showing that groups are working in many situations (Gendreau, 1996; Verdeyen, 1999).

One way to increase competence in group leading is to pair a skilled, experienced leader with an inexperienced one for a period of time and allow time for supervision after each session. In a relatively short time, unskilled leaders can get the experience they need to be able to lead interesting and helpful groups. Students, while still in school, may request the opportunity to co-lead with a more experienced leader and then lead some groups by themselves with supervision. Also, whenever possible, observe groups being led by competent leaders.

Not Planning

Having a plan is critical to making a group go well (Jacobs, Masson, and Harvill, 2002). Many leaders fail to plan their groups either because they do not take the time or they have never learned how to plan groups. Many make the mistake of thinking that planning is only deciding what movie to show or what topic to discuss. Leaders often fail to give additional thought to how to make sure the session is interesting and beneficial to the members. It is the leader's responsibility to plan the flow of the session and to consider discussion questions and activities that will make the group a valuable experience. Chapter 11 is devoted entirely to planning.

Example: Not Planning

The leader does not plan this meeting and, therefore, nothing meaningful is accomplished.

Leader: Let's start. Hopefully we won't spend more than an hour.
Kathy: What do we have to talk about?
Leader: Lots of things. We need to talk about three inmates, and some changes in the lunch schedule, if we have time. We always seem to fill the time.
Jeff: Speaking of time, weren't we supposed to get a clock for the recreation room?
Leader: Tina, weren't you going to get it?

Tina: I forgot. What kind was it again? Seems like someone wanted a certain kind. (*The group talks about the clock for ten minutes.*)

Leader: Okay, seems like we got the clock matter settled.

Jerry: What did we decide about inmates watching the Super Bowl?

Kathy: I am rooting for the Steelers! I grew up near Pittsburgh. Is anyone else rooting for the Steelers?

Sabera: I am a Cowboys fan, but they have been terrible lately. I also like the Browns.

In this group, the unskilled leader did not get to the important matters that needed to be discussed. The experienced leader would have planned the meeting to make sure important matters were discussed. His plan could have been something like:

- 5 minutes: Old and new business
- 40 minutes: Staffing of three inmates
- 10 minutes: Lunch schedule changes
- 5 minutes: Other business

Not Making the Group Meaningful—Just Filling Up Time

A common mistake is to allow group members to engage in discussion and activities that just fill up time. Some leaders give little thought to whether the discussion taking place is meaningful for the inmates. Untrained leaders conduct activities but make the mistake of not using the activities to lead to meaningful discussion, whereas an accomplished leader always pays attention to how meaningful the group is being and is flexible enough to change the direction of the group if what is happening is not being helpful for the members. Skilled leaders try hard to avoid the mistake of meaningless discussion and uninteresting and irrelevant activities.

Example: Discussion that Just Fills Up Time

This inexperienced leader is hoping the question gets members talking, which it does, but not about anything meaningful.

Leader: How are you feeling about not being home for Christmas?
Clev: I don't like Christmas.
Bret: I do and I am going to miss it. I am going to miss all the parties.
Al: My company used to have a big party. They served shrimp, lobsters, and all kinds of good food.
Joe: What kind of food will they serve us here?
Leader: I am not sure. I think it will be different from the regular meals.
Joe: Will we get anything special?
Butch: I don't like the new cook they hired. She makes things too hot.

In this example, the leader could have avoided this mistake by focusing the discussion since usually Christmastime generates some powerful feelings among inmates. After Bret's comment, the leader could have said, "What do you miss? Will you miss family or friends?" Or the leader could have said, "I realize some of you have children; does it bother you to not be home for Christmas?" By saying either of these, the leader would be trying to get members to share feelings that he knows exist for some, if not all, the members.

Example: Not Using Activities to Generate Valuable Discussion

The leader in this example makes the mistake of not getting the members to share more of their feelings that were generated during the movie.

Leader: So, what did you think of the movie?

Helen: I liked it. Sure made me think.

Monique: I liked it too, especially that scene with the mother and daughter.

Leader: Yeah, I think that is a powerful scene.

Dee: I thought it was a little overstated. People don't really act that way.

Leader: That may be. Any other thoughts? (*Pauses for a few seconds but becomes uncomfortable with the silence*) Let's do a different exercise. I've got this picture of an eagle I want you to look at. What is the first thing you think of?

The purpose of showing the movie was to generate meaningful discussion. In the example, the leader asks for reactions but does not try to elicit deeper thoughts and feelings. She then moves on to another exercise. The trained leader would word her comments differently because she would want to tap into the emotions that were aroused during the movie. (She has seen the movie and knows that it is powerful. During the movie she observes different members' reactions so that during the processing time she may choose to comment on the reactions she saw.) She could ask, "So, what scene moved you the most and why?" Also, after Monique's comment, the leader could have said, "I think that is a powerful scene. Let's talk about why that was so powerful. Monique, why was that scene meaningful for you?" A trained leader would not show a movie for ten-to-fifteen minutes and then spend less than two minutes talking about it.

Being Intimidated—Giving In to the Negative Members

A common mistake, especially for beginning group counselors, is being intimidated by the negative and often hostile members. In all correctional settings, some offenders will be negative. Some will try to control any group in which they are a member. Leaders should not be intimidated by these types of members, nor should leaders give in to the members in hopes that this will improve the group. Throughout the remainder of this book, we offer many suggestions and techniques that help to deal with these types of members. If you want to read more on this subject, Corey and Corey (2002) offer an in-depth look at dealing with difficult, negative members.

Example: Giving in to Negative Members

This group has eight members. Two negative members sway the leader.

Leader: (*In a flat voice*) How are things going today? I would like to do a quick check-in, then show this video on drugs and teenagers made by teenagers. What do you think of that idea?

Traci: I'm tired today. It's a nice day. We should go outside and be with nature.

Jean: That's a good idea. We need some time to chill out.

Leader: We did that on Monday.

Traci: Can't you see we're not into it?

The experienced leader would realize that he has a couple of negative members so he might start with the video, not giving the disruptive members any time to be negative. He would also use a more enthusiastic voice.

Not Interrupting Members

One of the most important skills for you to have when leading correctional groups is the ability to cut members off. This is also called "blocking" (Gladding, 2003). We all have been taught that interrupting or "cutting off" someone is rude, but in group leading, you must cut members off. It is a common mistake to let members ramble and hope that either they will eventually stop or some other member will cut them off. Also, at times, one member will attack another. To be successful, leaders have to be able to interrupt members.

Example: Leader Does Not Interrupt

The new inmate is rambling and the inexperienced leader is afraid of offending him, so he lets Larry go on and on.

Larry: This is my first group. I am nervous. I guess I should tell you about myself. I am from Texas. I grew up in a little town outside of Waco. I got in trouble because I lost my job and I knew how I could break into the place where I worked, so I did. I got away with it for the longest time. I think my cousin may have turned me in. He is this big Christian. I am not very religious. I did go to church when I was young.

Leader: I am not sure where you are going with all this.

Larry: I don't know. I talk a lot, especially when I am nervous. I did go back to church when I went to college. I went one year to North Texas. It is in Denton, Texas. In college I thought I wanted to study psychology but I partied way too much . . . . (*Ten minutes later, Larry stops. All the members have lost interest in the group.*)

The experienced leader would see that Larry was going to talk for a long time and that the members were getting bored. At any point after the leader tried to focus Larry, the mistake of letting Larry ramble could have been corrected by the leader interrupting and saying something like, (*with a kind voice*) "Larry, let me stop you. Do you want to take a minute or so more and tell about any feelings you are having about being here in prison or being in the group? I want to get started with our plan for today, but I do want to give you a chance to share your present feelings. If you do not want to share, that's fine."

Spotlighting Members When Trying to Draw Them Out

One of the major challenges of group work is getting members to talk. Experienced leaders are able to do this by using different strategies. A common mistake that inexperienced leaders make is that they cause members to become uncomfortable by putting them on the spot. Some leaders coerce the member to talk by calling on them and waiting for them to respond even though the member is very hesitant or fearful to share. This embarrasses the member and usually makes most of the other members uncomfortable.

Example: Spotlighting

Ned: I feel real guilty about what I did to my kids.

Don: I feel guilty about the pain I put my mom through.

Kevin: I feel guilty about so many things, especially some sexual stuff.

Leader: Gregg, you are always quiet. What do you feel guilty about? (*Gregg looks down and seems very nervous.*) Gregg, we'll just sit here until you talk. We've got lots of time.

In this example, the inexperienced leader embarrassed Gregg by focusing on him and then waited for him to share. This angers Gregg and the other members and causes members not to trust the leader. The skilled leader would probably ask if others want to share and could even call Gregg by name but then move on after a few seconds if it seemed apparent that Gregg did not want to share at this time.

Example: Spotlighting

This is an educational group and the leader sees that Cal is not paying attention.

Leader: Cal, what are your thoughts?

Cal: (*Negative voice*) Thoughts about what?

Leader: (*Condescending voice*) About what we were talking about.

Cal: What were you talking about?

Leader: That's my point. You have to pay attention to learn something!

Putting Cal on the spot certainly upsets Cal and usually some of the other members as well. In a case like this, where there is a negative member, the leader most likely would want to talk with him privately either during the session (pair up with him when putting members in pairs to discuss something) or sometime before the next session. The common mistake is to confront him in front of all the other members.

Responding to Every Comment

One of the hardest things to do in some groups is to stay quiet and let other members speak. A very common mistake of group leaders is to speak after each member talks. This is quite detrimental to the development of cohesion among the members and does not help in building trust. If the leader talks after each member talks, the members tend to feel connected to the leader but not to the other members. To get sharing and trust to develop, leaders have to make sure they do not always talk after each member speaks.

Example: Responding to Every Comment

This is a group for discussing fears and concerns the women have about when they will be out of prison. The leader feels compelled to speak after each member.

Judy: All I can think about is why did I do that? I knew better, but I was weak. I wanted Carlos to love me. I worry that I'll do something else stupid for a damn man's attention.

Leader: You aren't sure if you have enough strength to resist a man tempting you again?

Judy: I hope I do. I feel strong here, but there are no men here. I don't feel this is any kind of test for me.

Leader: What about all that you have learned in the classes and groups?

Judy: I do feel better about myself. I hate to admit it, but when my sister is here visiting and I am in the visiting room, something happens to me when I see a man giving me the eye.

Leader: What exactly do you think or feel when that happens?

Judy: I just get kind of excited, then mad at myself because it is men that got me in this mess in the first place.

Tammy: I am just the opposite. I look forward to getting a fresh start. I know I can be a better partner than I ever was. I was awful.

Leader: Why do you think you were awful?

Tammy: I would cheat on every guy I dated. I stole from most of them to support my habit. I really used men. I never enjoyed the sex.

Leader: What makes you think you will be different?

Tammy: I'm not into drugs now! That's a big thing. I do wonder if I can get to where I enjoy sex. I never had sex for the right reasons.

Leader: I think that's true for a lot of women. Tammy, talk some more about this.

In this example, the leader does not get the members to interact with each other but instead comments frequently. Her commenting every time a person speaks prohibits members from sharing and supporting one another. The skilled leader can avoid this mistake by being aware of the importance of sharing in a group like this one. Effective leaders will always monitor their tendency to speak after each member speaks. A much better group experience occurs when members feel comfortable sharing and asking questions of other members.

Not Having a Theory

In the first chapters of this book, we mentioned the value of knowing theories of human behavior. It is critically important for leaders to understand why people behave the way they do. Also, leaders need to know how to use theories in a practical way in a group to help the members who are struggling with painful issues that they cannot resolve. The highly skilled leader is able to teach group members how to use the theories to help themselves and other members. Unfortunately, many correctional workers do not understand the value of theory. As a result, their ability to help is greatly diminished. Walsh (2001) strongly believes in understanding the role that theories play in corrections. He devotes five chapters of his book on correctional counseling to understanding theories and their importance. Informed leaders use theories to understand offenders. They also use theories to help offenders express and deal with their deep-seated issues.

Example: Leader Not Knowing Theory

This is a treatment group dealing with addicted inmates.

> **Nan:** (*With head down, crying*) When I was doing drugs, I did all kinds of things that I am now so ashamed of. I turned tricks for dope and had two abortions. (*Sobbing*)
> **Leader:** What are your thoughts about Nan?
> **Candy:** I think Nan is nice. I appreciate all the things she does for me. She makes sure I get up and get moving each morning.
> **Sallie:** I gave two babies away because I know God frowns on abortions.

Because the leader does not know theory, she asks the group for their opinions. Unfortunately, the members have no idea how to help her, and say things that are nice but not helpful (Candy) or that are potentially harmful (Sallie). If the leader knew theory, she could help Nan dispute her negative self-talk. If the leader were well versed in theory, she could teach the members how to dispute their negative self-talk at the same time she was helping Nan. The value of theory in therapy groups cannot be overstated.

Not Involving Other Members When Working with a Member

Too often when a member brings up a problem, leaders mistakenly begin a one-on-one dialog with the member and do not include the other members. The other group members just sit and listen while the leader tries to help the one member. This often becomes boring and nonproductive for the other members. Sometimes it will be best for the leader to do the majority of the therapy, but the leader always should be aware of the other members. In most instances, the leader should try to actually include or mentally engage the other members when working with an individual member (Jacobs, Masson, and Harvill, 2002).

Example: Leader Not Involving Other Members

Nan: (*With head down, crying*) When I was doing drugs, I did all kinds of things that I am now so ashamed of. I turned tricks for dope and had two abortions. (*Sobbing*)

Leader: Nan, let me help you. You have to forgive yourself. All that was during your addiction. Let's look at your negative self-talk.

Nan: What do you mean?

Leader: It all has to do with what you are telling yourself.

Nan: Okay, I remember. But how does that apply to me?

Leader: (*Leader is only looking at Nan. The members are simply watching.*) You are obviously telling yourself things that aren't true. One thing is "I'm a terrible person."

Nan: But I am.

Leader: No, you aren't. You made some mistakes when you were active in your addiction.

The leader's mistake is conducting individual counseling almost as if the other members were just spectators.

Example: Leader Involving Other Members

Nan: (*With head down, crying*) When I was doing drugs, I did all kinds of things that I am now so ashamed of. I turned tricks for dope and had two abortions. (*Sobbing*)

Leader: (*With a very warm, kind voice*) Nan, let us help you. You have to forgive yourself. In fact, all of you need to forgive yourselves. Do some of you feel like Nan? (*Lots of heads nod.*) It all has to do with what you are telling yourself.

Candy: What do you mean?

Leader: Who remembers the ABC model we talked about last week?

Sallie: I do. That was all about how we cause ourselves pain. It is not events that cause it.

Nan: (*With much pain in her voice*) But I don't think that model can help me. My pain is too deep and is caused by all that bad stuff I did.

Leader: Nan, the model can help you. It can help everyone in this room. If anyone is still in pain, I want you to take a look at the negative self-talk that you are telling yourself. Nan, you are obviously telling yourself things that aren't true. (*To the group*) What do all of you think Nan is telling herself that is causing her pain?

In this example, the leader is using inclusive language and is getting the members involved in their own work and in Nan's work. This is much better than in the first example where the leader just did individual counseling.

Concluding Comments

In this chapter, we pointed out nine common mistakes that leaders make. If leaders can avoid or minimize these mistakes, they will be well on their way to being effective group leaders. By studying these mistakes, you can begin to understand why some groups you have led or observed were more successful than others. We suggest that you refer back to this list to evaluate yourself as you lead groups in the future.

Common Mistakes

- Allowing inexperienced or unskilled leaders to lead groups
- Not planning
- Not making the group meaningful—just filling up time
- Being intimidated—giving in to the negative members
- Not interrupting members
- Spotlighting members when trying to draw them out
- Responding to every comment
- Not having a theory
- Not involving other members when working with a member

Group Leadership Skills

The purpose of the first four chapters was to offer an introduction to groups in correctional settings. The remainder of the book focuses on skills, techniques, exercises, and other information that can help you to become a successful group leader. In this chapter, we discuss eleven leadership skills. The development of these skills is essential for effective group leading, and practice is crucial for mastery of these skills. Ideally, you are currently leading groups either in class or at work. If not, to practice the skills, we strongly encourage you to try using them in daily interactions with colleagues, family, and friends. Each of these eleven skills is necessary for becoming a skilled leader.

- Listening
- Summarizing
- Being aware of and manipulating the focus
- Holding the focus
- Shifting the focus
- Deepening the focus
- Generating energy
- Using eyes
- Using voice to set the tone
- Cutting off
- Drawing out

Listening

The ability to truly listen is essential for any counseling and is much more difficult when leading a group. The group leader has to listen to a number of people at one time, some who are talking and some who are communicating through nonverbal means. Many beginning leaders are able to listen to the person who is talking but fail to listen to the other group members. The skill is to listen to the person and also look around or glance at others to read how they are reacting to what is being said. Also, the skill includes listening (looking) for who is bored and who wants to speak next. Listening as a group leader is a skill that can be mastered, but it takes much practice. We recommend you practice this skill when interacting with a group of friends or family—try to pay attention to everyone and not just the person talking.

Summarizing

Many counselors have learned how to summarize what was said during their individual counseling sessions. Summarizing with groups is much more difficult because more happens with more people. The skilled leader is able to capture what has just happened not only with the person who just spoke but also with all that has been happening for the last few minutes. You can practice this skill by thinking how you would summarize what happened during some interaction between friends or family members or even from scenes in a movie or television show. The two following examples show how leaders can use the skill of summarizing.

Example One: Summarizing

Leader: Let me summarize the last few minutes. Johnny, you're saying you don't have a problem. Malik, you know you have a problem but don't care. Mike, you hate being here and want to make sure you never come back and you know drugs will lead you back here. Tom, you're not sure if you can stay clean once you leave here. You want to work on getting yourself stronger so that you won't be tempted by friends. Tom, let me say something about that and then we'll finish with the summary and move on to something else. I say this to you and to everyone. You probably are going to need to learn to make new friends who do not use drugs; otherwise, you will be back into drugs in no time. Bob, we don't know what you're thinking because you didn't seem like you wanted to share, but I was watching you and you seemed to be paying attention. Bob, I realize this is only your second day here, but we all hope you'll feel like sharing, even if it is just a little. In fact, at the end of group I will ask you to give us some of your thoughts and reaction to being here and being in the group.

Bob: Can I say something now?

Leader: Sure.

Example Two: Summarizing

This is a staff meeting regarding a teenager.

> **Leader:** Charlie, you feel strongly that Nieta should be moved up to another level because of how much she has improved. Melvin you don't think she should be moved because of her possible involvement in the incident the other night and the way she talked back to you. Ann, you don't feel strongly one way or the other, and James, you think she is ready for the next level. All I can say is, it usually is more clear-cut than this.

Being Aware of and Manipulating the Focus

During the session, it is very important for the leader to be aware of the focus of the group. To simplify this concept, we talk about the focus being either on a person, topic, or activity. For instance, when the focus is on a person, a member is talking about his issues, such as fears. When the focus is on a topic, most of the members are talking about their fears. When the focus is on an activity, each member is doing something, such as listing and ranking his or her fears. At any time, the focus is either on a person, topic, or activity. By being aware of the focus, the leader is able to decide to hold the focus, shift the focus, or deepen the focus. The decision to hold, shift, or deepen the focus is based on such things as the purpose of the group, the phase of the session, the amount of time left in the session, the level of interest the group has in the topic, the need for the person to talk, and the openness of the member who is talking. Leaders who are keenly aware of the focus will find that they are never lost and the group never gets away from them. They understand that they can shift the focus if necessary or hold the focus and deepen it if the member and group seem ready.

Holding the Focus

Holding the focus refers to keeping the attention or action of the group where it is rather than letting it shift or drift. In groups, it is easy for the discussion to start on one thing and within minutes be on something totally different. One key to effective group leading is to be able to hold the focus on important topics or hold the focus on a person when she is exploring her issues. Holding the focus is accomplished by bringing the focus back to the topic or person by redirecting the conversation. Often, the leader says something such as, "Let's focus on this issue until we get it resolved" or "Let's stay with Diane and see if we can help her resolve this problem with her mother."

Example One: Holding the Focus

Alexis: (*Crying*) I really do want to stop hating my mom, especially since she is dying, but I can't forgive her for what she did to me. She didn't believe me when I told her that Bob was doing stuff to me.

Leader: (*With a very kind, understanding voice*) We can help you to stop hating her but it is going to take your deciding that was then and this is now, like Carla did on Monday.

Alexis: I know, but it is hard to understand why she did that.

Carla: I am doing good with the stuff we worked on Monday, but there is another issue I realize I need to work on that may be even heavier. It has to do with my brother.

Leader: (*Holding the focus on Alexis; with a caring voice*) Carla, I'd like you to hold that until we finish working with Alexis. Let's stay with

Alexis right now. Alexis, what do you need to do so that you don't hate your mom?

Example Two: Holding the Focus

This is a task (staff) group meeting.

Cala: I think Brad should be sent away from here. This place is not equipped to handle guys like him.
Roy: But this is the first time he's ever done anything like that, and you know Big John is hard to work for.
Cala: Still, that's no excuse. I think we should notify someone today.
Phillipe: Big John is hard on these kids. How long has he been getting away with the crap he dishes out?
Leader: (*Holding the focus*) Let's first finish this about Brad. What do others of you think we should do about what happened?

To hold the focus, leaders often have to interrupt members who are going in another direction or who want the group to focus on them. Later in this chapter, we discuss the skill of cutting off, but we show it here in these examples since it is often the skill that is needed to hold the focus. If the leader cannot hold the focus, the group will go from topic to topic and person to person and be less useful. These next two examples further show the importance of holding the focus.

Example One: Holding the Focus through Cutting Off

This is a treatment group.

Omar: I can't understand why she doesn't write more. I want her to write everyday. Mail is a big deal for me. And when I yell at her about this, it just causes her to write less. I need help with this because I am so scared that I am going to lose her (*becomes tearful*).

Marty: Speaking of mail, I got a letter from my son. Now get this, he . . .

Leader: Hang on Marty. Let's get back to Omar. He seems to really be hurting.

Example Two: Holding the Focus through Cutting Off

This is in a town meeting on one of the units.

Winston: Somebody is taking the soap. There's none in the showers.

Tom: That's right. And I know it's my job to put soap out on Mondays and I do and it is gone by Wednesday.

Dick: I know I showered on Thursday and there was no soap. I had to go find some.

Abdul: I want to talk about the TV room. It is supposed to be quiet in there and people come in all the time and start carrying on and being loud. Football playoffs are coming up and . . . .

Leader: (*Interrupts*) Abdul, we'll get to the TV room later or at the next meeting. Let's first resolve this soap thing. How do we fix it?

Shifting the Focus

Being able to shift the focus is equally as important as being able to hold the focus. At times, a member or the group will get stuck on a topic and the leader will need to shift the focus to another person, topic, or activity. This often occurs when there is a member who likes attention and so tries to keep the focus on him, or when a topic is either not relevant to the purpose or when the discussion is no longer valuable to most members. It is the leader's responsibility to shift the focus. This is accomplished by interrupting and redirecting with a question or a statement.

Example One: Shifting the Focus Through Cutting Off

Phil: (*He's been talking a while.*) So, I think I got screwed. My lawyer didn't care and he didn't try to get me off. There was no one that could positively identify me, but he didn't care. If O. J. Simpson can get off, I should be able to. I plan to . . . .

Leader: (*Interrupting; Phil has talked about this in group at least two other times.*) Phil, there's nothing we can do about this, so I am going to shift to someone else. Who else has something they want help with?

Tray: I do. My son is coming for a visit next week for the first time.

Example Two: Shifting the Focus

At a staff meeting of probation officers, the focus has been on paperwork issues.

Donna: The paperwork is killing me. Lately, it seems that I treat paper as much as I treat people.

Jolene: Why do they keep changing it all the time? I get used to one form, and lo and behold, they change it!

Leader: (*Realizing two members have been on the subject of paperwork for about three minutes and some of the members are no longer paying attention, the leader decides to shift the focus.*) Since we can't resolve this, we ought to move on to some other matters. We need to figure out how we are going to handle Collette, and when are we going to start some additional groups?

Deepening the Focus

Deepening the focus means getting members to explore things below the superficial or surface level so that the members get new insights or information. Deepening the focus is an essential skill for group leading and is more important for some types of groups than others. For task and administrative groups, holding the focus is often what is important and the leader generally would not try to take the members to deep emotional levels. For educational groups, the leader would try to deepen the focus to the point where information is meaningful and helpful to the members. With treatment groups, the leader definitely should try to deepen the focus to the point where some, if not all of the members, can gain some personal insights.

One way we look at deepening the focus is through the use of the Depth Chart, an idea first described in *Impact Therapy* (Jacobs, 1994). In the Depth Chart, 10 represents addressing the surface of a topic and 1 means going very deeply into the issue or topic. Group sessions can be charted on this scale. Groups that stay mainly on the surface would go 10, 9, 8, then to a new topic, 10, 9, 8, then to another topic, 10, 9, 8. Below is a Depth Chart drawing of group where the members never went below an 8. They start talking about issues with their parents, then they switch to superficially talking about drug use, and then they switch to surface thoughts about guilt.

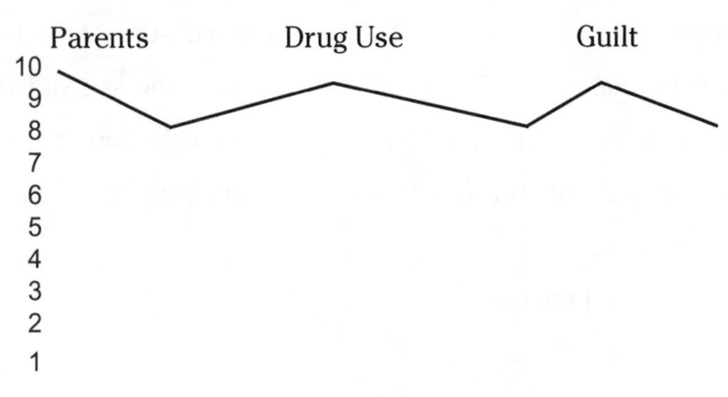

When the leader is able to deepen the focus, the session goes to 7, 6, 5, or even deeper. The ultimate aim of most educational and treatment groups is to hold and deepen the focus so that the group goes below 7 on the Depth Chart and there is impact—a longer lasting form of understanding or insight—more than just hearing something.

In the example below, the leader is deepening the focus on Tim. She uses the members and her questions to get Tim to go below 7. Tim begins to really think about change and he is not just telling stories or complaining.

Example: Deepening the Focus

Other members have been sharing and Tim joins in the discussion.

Tim: I don't see any way that my life can work. This is who I am and there's nothing anyone can do about it.

Leader: Tim, that's not true. There are plenty of things you can do about it. All the people in this group can do some things that will make their lives better. Joe is doing that by speaking up more, and Bobby is certainly doing better with his anger. (*Trying to get Tim to go deeper*) Let me ask you this, why does your life always have to be bad?

Tim: What do you mean? It just always has.

Leader: I know your life has been a mess, but my question is, does it always have to be a mess? Can you learn some new things? (*Tim seems to really be listening and thinking.*) Let me ask all the others, do you think Tim's life has to always be chaotic and traumatic? Raise your hand if you think it has to. (*No hands go up.*) Tim, none of us think it has to.

Tim: How do I change it?

Leader: Any of you have some ideas?

Joe: Tim, you have to get out of the little child seat (*Points to small child's chair that the leader uses in the group to represent the Child ego state from Transactional Analysis theory.*) [Transactional Analysis is discussed in Chapter 6.]

Danny: Tim, you do great for a while, and then a letter from home comes, and you lose it. I think you need to work through lots of issues about that.

Tim: I know.

Leader: What we're saying is, this can be done.

Tim: (*In a very thoughtful voice*) You are right. I am in the child seat a lot and when I am, I don't think. It is such a habit.

The Depth Chart for the example above would look something like this:

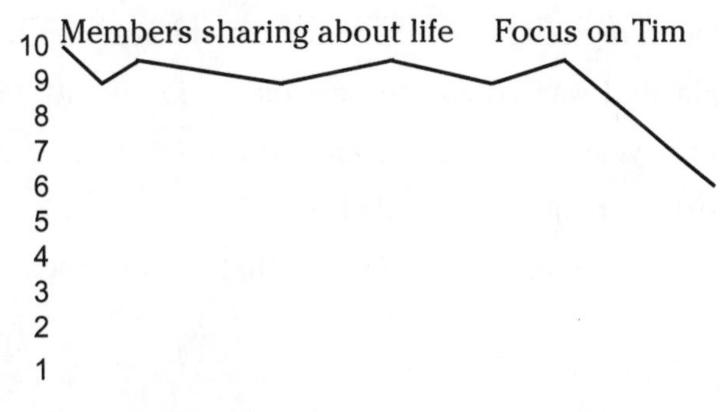

Unskilled leaders lead groups that have a pattern of 10, 9, 8, then 10, 9, 8, then 10, 9, 8—that is jumping from topic to topic. Not being able to hold and deepen the focus allows for a 10, 9, 8; 10, 9, 8 pattern which is one that has little impact. An example of this would be as follows:

Example: Not Deepening the Focus

Leader: When do you think your problems started?

Al: I think my problems started with school. I wasn't very smart and was made fun of.

Phil: My dad was always in trouble with the law. He would show me things he had stolen. It's all I have known.

Marko: I had this girlfriend who wanted me to get her things all the time, like jewelry and stuff, so I started stealing. I did get her some nice things, but when I went to jail the first time, she dumped me. What a bitch. She's now married to this banker guy.

Hector: Mine started when I started smoking weed. I got with the wrong crowd and dropped out of football. I wish I'd never done that. I could have played in college, and I always wanted to be an architect but that will never happen.

Kevin: I played basketball until I got drunk one night before a game and was kicked off the team.

Leader: Did others of you play sports?

Al: I played baseball up until I started doing drugs and the games interfered with my drug time. I actually could have been a very good baseball player. I was voted the best player in my Little League for three straight years, but starting around age fourteen drugs became more important to me. Drugs and girls.

Leader: Let's talk about sex. When did that start happening for each of you?

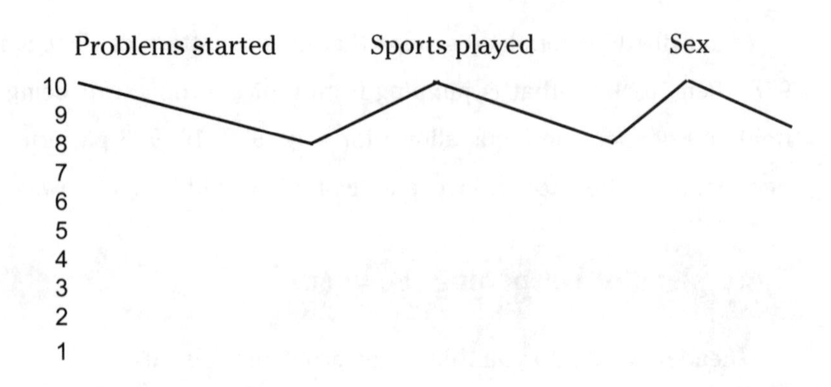

Here, the leader starts on a topic and then goes to other topics without taking the session to any meaningful level. Not deepening the focus is a common mistake of beginning leaders. The skilled leader could have deepened the focus in many different areas. He could have helped the members connect the past to the present and helped them to see that they could change their future. He could have focused on Hector wanting to be an architect and explored how he could still do that. He could have deepened the focus on how much drugs, alcohol, and sex played a part in getting them in trouble.

Treatment group leaders should always be thinking about when and how to deepen the focus because groups that go below 7 get the members thinking or get members to finish unfinished business that they have. In fact, the reason why they are called treatment groups is because the members need to explore issues and feelings at a deeper level. All treatment and most education groups should go below 7 on the Depth Chart.

Generating Energy

Leaders of groups in correctional settings must be able to generate interest and energy in the group because most of the time the members will not do this. Remember, these members are mainly in a group because they are in jail or prison and generally are not that interested in personal growth and awareness. They are also not particularly interested in extending themselves or being cooperative. Therefore, it is always the leaders' responsibility to try to interest the members in topics and discussions that are beneficial to them. Some educators advocate that it is the members' responsibility, but we have found that members most often do not generate meaningful or beneficial discussions, so we encourage leaders to always plan interesting and energizing topics and activities. *Do not put the responsibility of generating energy on your members.*

Using Eyes

Looking around the group is very important for the group leader because it enables the leader to see how members are reacting to what is being said or done in the group. By looking around, leaders can pick up on who seems eager or ready to talk, who seems withdrawn, who seems annoyed, and so forth. It is essential that leaders are always seeing how members are responding during the session.

Not only should leaders look around when they are speaking, but they also should glance around when a member is speaking. Most leaders make the mistake of looking only at the member who is talking, which is another hard-to-break, deeply ingrained rule from growing up. This causes two problems: one, the member talking will look primarily at the leader and two, the leader is not picking up others' reactions to what is being said. Looking around while another is talking may sound easy, but actually this is one of the more difficult skills to master. It is important in the first few sessions for leaders to explain why they will not always be staring at group members when they are speaking.

Example: Using Eyes

Leader: Joe, you may have noticed that when you were talking, I did not look just at you.

Joe: I did notice that. Why weren't you listening to me?

Leader: Let me explain my looking around to all of you. When you are talking, I will be listening, but I will be scanning the group periodically to see people's reactions. My responsibility is to pay attention to everyone. By looking around, I get a sense of who is interested, who wants to talk, and who seems bored. Also, my looking around should signal you to look at others and not just at me.

To master the skill of using your eyes effectively, you should observe yourself and others and see how people often just look at one person when talking. Try to practice looking around when talking and when others are talking. Notice how much information you pick up when you look for nonverbal reactions. As you become better at this, you will gather more information with shorter, darting glances and it will seem natural and less obvious.

In addition to leaders using their eyes effectively, leaders also want to encourage group members, when talking, to look at each other. The natural tendency of members is to look at the leader, but making eye contact with others helps to build cohesion in a group. Another reason for having members look around is that they benefit from seeing the facial reactions and head nods of the other members rather than imagining how others are reacting. It is valuable for members to see others who seem to agree or understand, and it is also helpful for members to experience negative feedback or reactions that disagree with their own.

Using Voice to Set the Tone

Most beginning leaders do not understand the value of using their voice effectively. Leaders often do not consciously learn how to use their voice to set the tone for their groups. Talking energetically sets one tone; talking in a slow, deliberate way sets another tone. A leader's voice also communicates a level of caring and seriousness so it is very important that leaders be aware of the pattern of their voice. A leader who speaks in a monotone tends to put people to sleep. A varied and passionate tone encourages people to think and feel. If you have not given much thought to how voice can affect a group, we suggest that you practice using different voice patterns and note the effect that each voice pattern has on people. In the examples in this book, we often make reference to the voice pattern of the leader and the members to emphasize its importance. (Use of voice to set the tone is also discussed in Chapter 12.)

Cutting Off

Cutting off is essential for being able to lead an effective group since this skill allows the leader to control the group. (The term "cutting off" is also referred to by some group leaders as "interrupting" or "blocking." We use all these terms in this book to refer basically to the same skill.) Cutting off means stopping a member from talking. In groups, the need for cutting off occurs often and for various reasons.

- Interrupting is needed when another member brings up a subject that is not relevant to what is being said or tries to shift the focus to his own topic.
- Blocking is needed when a member gets excited and wants to talk even though another member is talking.
- Cutting off is needed when a member wants to dominate the group.
- Interrupting is needed when a member wants to give long-winded answers or explanations. (This happens frequently in prison groups.)
- Cutting off is needed when a member attacks another member.
- Cutting off is needed when a member wants to preach to the group.

Of the skills we discuss in this book, cutting off is the skill that most leaders either are uncomfortable with or they do it in such a way as to cause animosity toward themselves as the leader. When interrupting, the leader has to pay particular attention to her voice because the member being cut off can easily be offended by the intervention, especially if it is done in a harsh, abrupt manner.

The leader who is comfortable and skillful at cutting off has a much greater chance of directing the focus of the group. A leader who has good cut-off skills can hold the focus when a member jumps in and tries to take over or direct the discussion away from what is currently happening. That is, the leader can cut off the interrupting or eager member. The leader who is keenly aware can cut off quickly and more subtly. You can develop a higher level of comfort using cutting-off techniques by practicing them in groups or in social situations where the conversation seems to be wandering and you try to bring the conversation back to the subject.

Example One: Cutting Off

The leader uses cutting-off skills to hold the focus on a member.

> **Terry:** I hate being here and I fear what I will do if I can't get a better attitude. I need some major help. I thought I would adjust but it has been over a month and things aren't better.
>
> **Troy:** I have been feeling better lately. Ever since my girlfriend came and swore she would wait for me, I have felt better. I still do wonder if she loves me. I . . . .
>
> **Leader:** (*Interrupting with a kind voice*) Troy, I want us to stay with Terry. He really does seem to want our help.

Example Two: Cutting Off

A leader will use cutting-off skills to shift the focus when a member is going on and on about some topic that is boring the other members.

> **Randy:** I gambled on everything. Football season kept me busy, especially lately with games on Monday, Tuesday, Thursday and all of the weekend. Basketball was harder for me to master. What am I saying? I really didn't master any of it. But basketball was harder because one player . . . .

Leader: Randy, we're focusing on current feelings. Let us hear from others while you think about how you feel now about all the gambling. Justin, what are your thoughts?

Example Three: Cutting Off

A leader will use cutting off to deepen the focus when a member is willing to delve deeper into his issue but is staying on the surface regarding his thoughts or feelings.

Healy: I have such anger at all kinds of people. I hate the guy that got me started using! He was this older guy—I was only fourteen. I was amazed that he liked me and then . . .

Leader: (*With a serious, thought-provoking voice*) Healy, what do you need to do to get rid of all your anger?

Healy: (*With tears*) I don't know, but it's killing me. I need some help.

In the first session of the group, it is important that the leader tell the group that at times he will be cutting off members. This helps avoid misinterpretation or hurt and angry feelings that could occur as a result of the leader interrupting a member. The leader should tell the members that it is his responsibility to pay attention to all the members, and there will be times when he may feel that he needs to stop a member for one reason or another. The leader should talk about cutting off during the first session and then remind the members periodically that he will be doing this. Being able to cut off gives the leader confidence that no member will take over the group, nor will any member be hurt by another member, because the leader knows she can use her skills to stop any attacks or harmful comments.

Drawing Out

An extremely important leadership skill in groups in correctional settings is drawing out members, because so many are nonvoluntary and are not used to talking in front of other people. In Chapter 4, we discussed a number of common mistakes. Included in that list was "spotlighting," which occurs when a leader does a poor job of trying to draw out a member. Instead of feeling helped to talk, the member feels pressured to talk because the leader has singled him out. Leaders need to learn how to draw out members without them feeling spotlighted.

Forcing members to talk is rarely a good thing and often is harmful to the dynamics in a group. Forced comments end up being superficial and do not add to the discussion. The challenge for leaders is to figure out ways to get members to want to talk and share relevant and meaningful thoughts about the issues being discussed. Also, when members are forced to talk, they often feel singled out or picked on. One way to minimize a person feeling this way is to never call on one person and then just wait until he or she speaks. We suggest you "gently nudge" members by calling on one, waiting for just a second or two, then calling on a second person. This way, neither person feels on the spot.

Example: Drawing Out

Leader: (*With a soft, inviting voice and eyes focused on Dave*) Dave, you haven't talked about your fears. Do you want to share? (*Pause for a couple of seconds; Dave is looking uncomfortable.*) Hector, we haven't heard from you, either. Do either you or Dave want to add anything?

In this example, the leader waits to see if either Hector or Dave seem as if they want to speak. If not, the leader would move on to someone else and not try to purposely make Dave and Hector feel uncomfortable. The important thing is to not spotlight members by putting pressure on them to speak.

The use of drawing out does not apply only to those who are quiet. The skill refers to getting members to share. Many times leaders will need to draw out members who are waiting their turn to share. One of the easiest ways to draw out members is by observing if they seem ready to talk and then asking them for comments. Members will send nonverbal cues such as making eye contact, changing their facial expression, taking in a sharp breath, or shifting their posture. Each of these often indicates a readiness to speak. Members who want to talk will not feel spotlighted if the leader calls on them. The leader's effective use of her eyes will help greatly in appropriately drawing people out. Too often, leaders who are not using their eyes effectively call on people randomly instead of observing their readiness to talk. This not only causes discomfort, but also can cause members to dislike the leader.

Leaders can use a number of ways to get members to share in groups without spotlighting them. We discuss three here: rounds, written exercises, and movement exercises. These are discussed in more detail in Chapter 8, but are specifically included her because of their effectiveness in drawing out individuals without spotlighting.

Rounds. Rounds are very helpful in getting members to speak. The round consists of going around the group and having each person say a word, number, or brief comment about something such as how his week was, how he would rate his stay at the jail, and so forth. By asking each person to give a very brief answer, no one feels singled out and usually everyone will share something. Often, rounds help to draw out the quiet member because the leader can come back to that member and ask her what she meant by her rating or comment.

Example: Use of Rounds to Draw Out

Leader: Let's do a round about how committed you are to working hard in this group. On a 1-10 scale, with 10 being willing to work very hard and 1 not at all, where are you?

Sarah: 7

Shannon: 3

Bonita: 5

Deb: 8

Iona: 3

Leader: Bonita, why is it just a 5?

Bonita: I've just been through all this before and don't have faith I can be strong enough. It's not about this group but more about me.

Leader: (*Knowing Iona has rarely talked in the group but seems like she is paying attention.*) Iona, what is your 3 about?

Iona: All of this is new and scary to me. I don't have enough trust to share anything personal.

Deb: I felt that way, but one day thought what do I have to lose?

Written Exercises. Written exercises, such as making a list or completing a few sentence stems, help draw out members because all persons have a written answer if the leader calls on them. Members can then read what they wrote if the leader calls on them, and they do not usually feel on the spot because they have their answers in front of them. Especially in correctional settings, leaders should make sure the members can read and write because they do not want to embarrass them. If the leader knows they cannot read or write, he can help them or give them the option of just thinking of their answers.

Example: Use of Written Exercise to Draw Out

Leader: Let's hear what you wrote. The first question was what is the hardest thing about being in prison? (*Looking around seeing, that Elias seems ready to talk*) Elias, what did you answer?

Elias: The boredom and no privacy.

Leader: Sam?

Sam: Thinking about how long I have to be here.

Leader: (*To draw out Amos who has been very quiet the entire session*) Amos, what did you put?

Amos: The hardest thing for me is missing my family, and they are so far away.

Movement Exercises. Certain movement exercises are also good for drawing out members because the members "speak" by moving to different parts of the room. A good movement exercise for drawing out members is the "wall-to-wall continuum." This exercise consists of having one wall represent one position, such as "hard worker" and the other wall represent the opposite, such as "lazy." Starting lined up behind one another in the middle of the room, group members are asked first to think about where they would place themselves to represent their position along a continuum from one wall to the other and then to move to that spot in the room and stand there. By having members move to where they see themselves on the continuum, each member is sharing. They are just doing it with their feet and not their mouths. The leader draws members out by asking questions about why they put themselves where they did. Most members will be willing to share and are very interested in where others placed themselves. Some examples of these would be happy—sad; winner—loser; leader—follower; lots of guilt—little guilt.

Example: Use of Movement Exercise to Draw Out

Leader: I want all of you to come to the middle of the room and line up behind Pam. The wall on the right represents lots of guilt and the wall on the left represents no guilt about what you did. On the count of three, I am going to ask you to move to the point where you see yourself. On three you move. Ready? One, two, three. (*Everyone moves.*)

Leader: Toni, why did you put yourself way over on the guilt side?

Toni: (*In a very pained voice*) Because I hate myself for what I did to my parents.

Leader: Brandi, what about you?

Brandi: I am feeling pretty good now. A year ago, I would have been way over there—tons of guilt.

Leader: (*Wanting to draw out Dawn*) Dawn, you put yourself in a spot with lots of guilt. What is going on about that?

Dawn: I try not to think about what I did. When I do it is so painful. (*Starts to cry*) I don't know how I am going to live with myself. At least with drugs I was numb.

Leader: Are you willing to let us try to help?

Dawn: I think so.

Concluding Comments

In this chapter we discussed eleven important skills: listening, summarizing, being aware of and manipulating the focus, holding the focus, shifting the focus, deepening the focus, generating energy, using eyes, using voice to set the tone, cutting off, and drawing out. These skills are useful in every group session, and your level of ability to use them will directly influence your success as a leader. Leaders who master these skills can enjoy the challenge of leading groups in correctional settings.

Use of Theories

In Chapter 2, we mentioned the importance of knowing theories when leading treatment groups. Counseling theories help explain why people do what they do. Groups on anger, addictions, denial, relapse, or anxiety will only be effective if the leader can use theory to help members understand their thoughts, feelings, and behaviors. Leaders who conduct treatment groups will want to be able to listen to various issues with a theoretical ear. Leaders need to be able to teach the members theories that they can use in the group and in their daily lives. For leaders who plan to only lead administrative, task, and basic educational groups, knowing counseling theories will not be as important, but all treatment groups definitely require that the leaders have some theoretical knowledge.

In this chapter, we discuss three theories that are very helpful in correctional settings. We do not go into great detail about any of these because we believe that most readers will have had a theories course during their undergraduate or graduate education or they will seek out books on the specific theories that they find most interesting. Those who feel weak in theory may want to start their reading with *The Theory and Practice of Group Counseling* (Corey, 2000), which gives an overview of theories and shows how they are used in group counseling.

Rational Emotive Behavior Therapy (REBT)

Rational Emotive Behavior Therapy (REBT) is a cognitive-behavioral theory that Albert Ellis originated in the late 1950s. It is currently one of the leading theories used in counseling (Ellis and Dryden, 1997). A number of people have used Ellis' work or developed ideas similar to his (Beck and Weishaar, 1995; Lombardo and Smith, 1996; Maultsby, 1984; Ross, Fabiano, and Ewles, 1988). These theories are similar to Rational Emotive Behavioral Therapy, which is built on the premise that thoughts cause feelings and that people cause themselves problems by what they continually tell themselves about events or people. That is, it is not what happens (being in prison) nor is it a person (the spouse, the parent, the warden, another inmate, the other gang, or the judge) that upsets a person, but rather it is what that person tells himself about the event or person that causes him to become and stay upset. The theory can be presented in a simple ABC format to inmates:

A = the activating event or person

B = the beliefs or self-talk

C = the consequence, which can be a feeling, a behavior, or both a feeling and a behavior

Most people believe that A causes C but really it is B, the self-talk, that causes C. For example, it is not being in prison (A) that is causing the person to be angry, but rather, what he is telling himself, (B) such as "I don't deserve this!! (C) The judge was out to get me. He had no right to give me a prison sentence!" It is this kind of self-talk that is causing the emotional reaction, and not the fact the person is in prison. This can explain why some inmates react quite differently to incarceration; they have a different set of sentences as B. Teaching group members that they can change their feelings by changing their thoughts can be very helpful. Members can learn this model quickly and can use it to help other members when they are struggling with different emotions, like anger, guilt, or shame.

If you never have been exposed to REBT, you may want to stop and think about what you believe about where feelings come from. Certainly in treatment groups you are going to be trying to help inmates figure out what is causing their intense feelings. Take a minute and reflect on how you would answer the question, "Where do my feelings come from?"

Example One: REBT

Leader: I want to talk about your plans for Christmas day. Any thoughts or feelings?

Dee: (*In a very sad, depressed voice*) I am not going to get out of bed. How am I supposed to feel? I am in jail and some other woman is going to be with my kids during Christmas. They are going to forget me, I just know it.

Leader: (*With an empathetic voice*) Dee, we know it is painful for you.

Sherece: I feel the same way she does.

Leader: I know that some of you feel this way. In fact, that is why I brought up the subject. Let me show you something that may help you. It is an ABC model, which applies to all situations, not just Christmas. Some of you believe that it is the event, that is, not being with your kids during Christmas, which I call A, that is causing C, the feeling of great sadness or depression. (*The leader writes this on the chalkboard.*)

A. Event = Not being with kids during Christmas

B.

C. Feeling = extreme sadness, depressed

Leader: Most of you believe that A is causing C, right?

Joanie: Yeah, I want to be with my kids. I want to do a tree with them. Last year we had the best Christmas ever!

Leader: No doubt most, if not all, of you would like to be with your kids, except Candy, since you don't have kids. Candy, you can apply this to other situations or Christmas in general.

Candy: That's fine. I'd like to see you help Dee because she has been so down lately. I am worried about her.

Leader: Dee, this can help if you use it. This can help all of you. In fact, this ABC model helped me when my mother died. Anyone know what B is? (*The leader pauses and there is silence—the members are thinking,but no one answers.*) B stands for the beliefs or self-talk that is going on in your head about A. In other words, it is B that causes C, and not A that causes C.

Dee: If they would let me out of here for Christmas, I would feel fine! There's nothing in my head.

Leader: You would be happier if you were able to leave, but you are not going to. In fact, no one here is going to get to be home at

Christmas. Some of the women will feel a little down and some will be totally miserable. What is the difference?

Lucy: They have been here longer?

Joanie: Maybe this place is better than where they come from?

Leader: No, it has to do with their self-talk. If you say, "I can't stand it! This is awful. My kids will forget me!" Then, you will feel very sad and depressed. Right? (*Writes on the board*)

A. Event = Not being with kids during Christmas

B. Beliefs/Self-talk-
I can't stand it!
This is awful.
My kids will forget me!

C. Feeling = extreme sadness, depressed

Leader: Can you see that it is the self-talk and not the event that is causing the feelings? (*Members are staring at the board. Some nod yes.*) If it is the event, then everyone would have to be equally as upset, and most of you are not. My point is that we cause ourselves to feel the way we do. People or events do not make us feel anything, but rather, it is what we tell ourselves.

Dee: How do I change my feeling?

Leader: By changing your self-talk. (*To the group*) Do you think Dee can stand being here over Christmas?

Candy: She's not going to like it, but she can stand it. She has to.

Leader: That's right, Dee. If you tell yourself, "I don't like it, but I can stand it," do you think you would feel better?

Dee: But my kids are going to forget me.

Leader: Dee, I know you are telling yourself that but there is no proof that this will happen. In fact, even kids who have never met their biological parents due to them being in prison think about them. From what you have told us, your kids certainly have their share of good memories of you. Also, there are things you can do that will make sure they do not forget you. We'll come back to that in a minute. For all of you, can you stand being here? (*Heads nod yes.*) Dee, can you stand it?

Dee: Well, I guess. I have to.

Leader: Can you see how changing your self-talk, can change how you feel?

Lucy: You're saying we can change our self-talk. But isn't that lying to yourself?

Leader: No, it's about telling yourself the truth.

In this example, the leader would continue to help Dee and others dispute their self-talk. The leader would involve the other members when working with Dee whenever possible and encourage the other members to apply the model to their own situations. It is obvious the leader believes in Rational Emotive Behavioral Therapy, better known as REBT, and knows the theory well. She has planned to use this model in the remaining group sessions since it is one that the members can understand and follow fairly easily.

Example Two: REBT

In this example, the leader has asked the question about what makes people angry. All the inmates answered and Tim has been talking about how out of control he is with his anger.

Leader: Tim, would you like some help with controlling your anger?

Tim: It's just who I am.

Leader: No, it's what you are telling yourself.

Tim: Bull!

Leader: (*With a warm, inviting voice*) No, you are upsetting yourself. Others of you are upsetting yourselves as well. That's why I asked the question about what makes you mad. It is not true that James' wife is making him mad or Phil's judge is making him mad. Let me tell you about something that can help all of you. It is a simple model, something I learned a few years ago that really changed my life. I learned that it is my thoughts that cause my feelings, not other people. I used to think the warden upset me or my wife made me mad, but I learned this ABC model at a workshop and it has made so much difference in my life.

James: So, you don't think your wife makes you mad?

Leader: I know she doesn't. It is what I tell myself about my wife's behavior that upsets me. I upset myself.

Phil: How's that possible? If she goes to a lunch with another man, you're saying you wouldn't be mad?

Leader: I may be angry, but I know she's not causing it. I am. All she is doing is going to lunch. At that workshop where I learned this, it became clear to me that I am in charge of my feelings, not others. I can control my feelings by controlling my thoughts.

Elvin: But she's causing you to think things!

Leader: Let's take the example of my wife going to lunch with a man she works with. Here's what my self-talk might be: She has no right to do that! She's going to leave me. She doesn't love me. She's my wife and she should not talk with other men! (*Goes to the whiteboard and writes:*)

Self-Talk
She has no right to do that!
She's going to leave me.
She doesn't love me.
She's my wife and she should not talk with other men!

Leader: If I tell myself those things, then I will be upset, angry, and really deep-down worried. What I do now is challenge my self-talk. This actually happened a few weeks ago—my wife went to lunch with this old high-school friend of hers. Did it mean she didn't love me or she was going to leave me? Heck no. I have to admit I had those thoughts, but I challenged them. She actually called me to tell me she was going to do it just in case someone saw her and called me. She told me not to worry. The guy was in town on business and they are in the same business—advertising. Later, she told me they went to lunch and talked about her life, his life, business, and old times. I asked her if she had feelings for him, and she laughed. All I can say is, I stayed calm because I challenged the self-talk in my head. I have to say I had all those thoughts, but I did what I learned at the workshop—I challenged my self-talk as to whether the sentences were true.

Tim: Are you saying I cause my anger?

Leader: That is exactly what I am saying. You told us that your brother is making you so angry because he's not helping your family out. Tim, your brother is not making you angry. All he is doing is behaving. You are making yourself angry.

In this example, the leader is teaching the members the principles of REBT: Thoughts cause feelings; we upset ourselves by what we tell ourselves. The leader does a good job of presenting the model by using his own situation. The leader would then help members explore their own self-talk that is causing them to get angry and he would help the members dispute their irrational self-talk. This concept of thoughts causing feelings would have to be reiterated from session to session before members would thoroughly grasp it.

Example Three: REBT

Leader: Phil, what happened yesterday at your hearing?

Phil: (*Very upset*) I got turned down.

Tim: (*Who really has taken to REBT*) What are you telling yourself?

Phil: Those bastards. They saw where two years ago I got in trouble, but hell, since then I have been completely good! And my wife, she was mad at me when I told her. I'm pissed about that as well!

Tim: Those are the feelings; what are you saying to yourself?

Phil: I don't know.

Leader: Would you like to feel differently?

Phil: Yes.

Leader: What does Phil need to do to feel differently?

Elvin: Change his self-talk.

James: Turn down the volume on some of his self-talk.

Tim: I think he's saying "This is awful and I can't stand it!"

Leader: Is this right?

Phil: It is awful.

Leader: Remember the ABC model. What is the event?

Tim: Sounds to me like there are two events—being turned down for parole and his wife's reaction.

Leader: (*To the group*) Does that seem right? (*They nod.*) Which of these do you want help with first?

Phil: I guess the parole thing. That really has me upset.

James: Phil, remember, you are upsetting yourself. Most of us have been through what you have been through on this parole thing. We just want to help you change all the illogical, not-true self-talk.

In this example, the group would continue to use REBT to help Phil with his two situations. By involving the other members, it helps to further their belief and understanding of the model and it allows the leader to not be the only one doing the therapy.

These examples show how the theory can be used with group members. For those who like this theory and want to learn more about it, we suggest you read *A Practitioner's Guide to Rational Emotive Therapy* (Walen, DiGiuseppe, and Dryden, 1992). This is an excellent book about Rational Emotive Behavioral Therapy and how to use it with clients and group members. A useful web site for more information about REBT and a catalog of books and tapes is *www.rebt.org*.

Transactional Analysis—TA

Transactional Analysis (TA) was originated by Eric Berne in the late 1950s and early 1960s. It is an excellent theory to help individuals understand themselves with special emphasis on understanding their interactions with other people. Since many inmates are not very self-aware and often have conflicts with other inmates, their family, and friends, TA is an excellent model to teach in a correctional setting. When inmates realize that they are coming from one of the three ego states and have a choice as to which one they come from, many start seeing that their habits and negative behaviors can be understood and changed. Most inmates pay attention and find TA to be attention-grabbing when it is being taught or being used because it can be presented in a highly visual way with drawings or with chairs. On numerous occasions we have gotten feedback from workshop participants regarding the tremendous positive value of TA in their groups in prisons and other correctional settings. We believe that more research is needed regarding TA and other theories that are being used in individual and group counseling. Some studies were done in the 1970s on TA groups in correctional settings (Adams, 1974; Jesness, 1975; Nicholson, 1970) although no recent studies of TA have been reported.

Berne talks about three ego states: Parent, Adult, and Child. The theory is often presented using visual images:

The Parent part can be divided into two parts—the Nurturing Parent and the Critical Parent. The Child also can be divided into two parts—the OK Child (or Free Child) and the Not OK Child. The key to helping inmates is for them to come to understand each of these five parts.

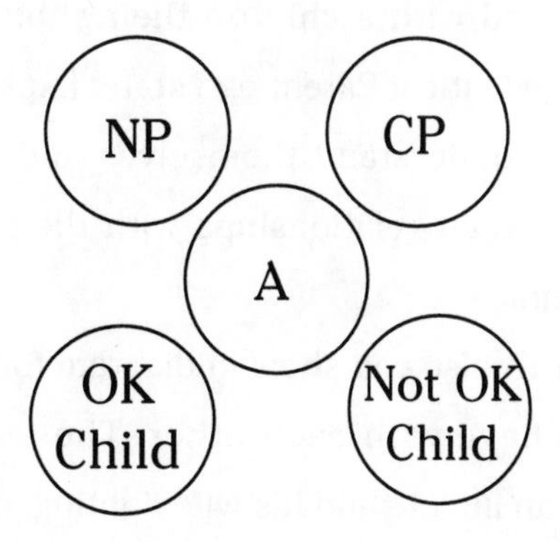

The way a person interacts with others depends on how large or small each of these parts is. Problems come up in individuals' lives if they let their Critical Parent or their Not OK Child dominate the Adult part. The

Adult is the logical, thinking part of a person. The drawings below show an Adult contaminated by the Critical Parent and an Adult contaminated by a Not OK Child. TA therapists use the term "contaminated" when an individual is not thinking clearly from his or her Adult due to the presence of either the Child or Parent ego states. When a person's Adult is ruled by some other ego state, that individual tends to have interactions that are not effective. The person whose Adult has been contaminated by the Critical Parent will usually hear things as negative and will send out negative messages most of the time. The person whose Adult is contaminated by their Child often will feel hurt or rejected when interacting with others.

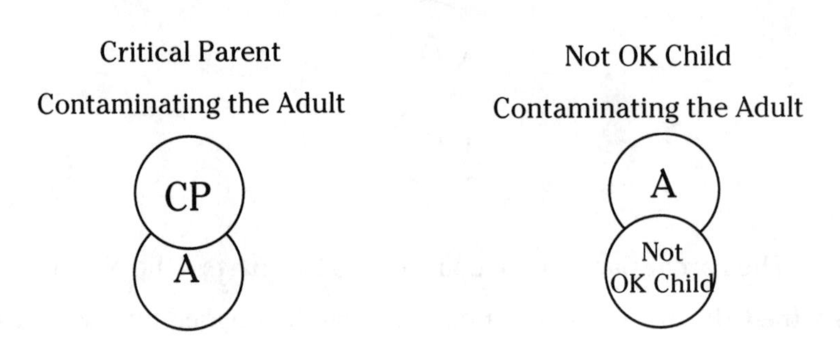

Inmates with low self-esteem have large Not OK Child ego states. Inmates who walk around with a chip on their shoulder or who like to boss others have a large Critical Parent ego state. Explaining this model to inmates can help them understand themselves and any fights they are having at the prison or their relationships with their spouse, lover, children, parents, and friends.

Leaders who use TA also can show in diagram form the transactional patterns that people have with each other. The leader can draw, for instance, a diagram of an inmate and his wife fighting. It might look like the following:

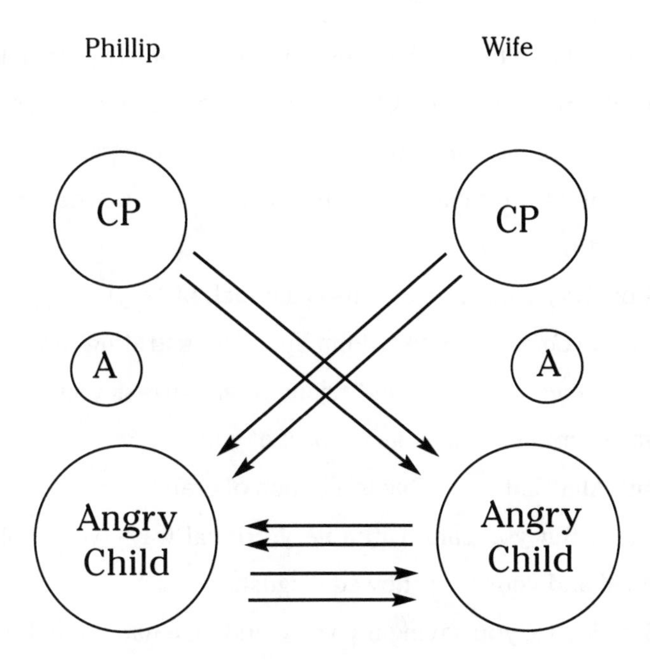

If you are not familiar with TA, you may want to take a few minutes and think about your own ego states and which parts are large and which are small. Also, you may want to think about how your Adult might be contaminated by other parts. If you currently have conflicts with people in your life, you may want to reflect on how you would draw those conflicts using the TA model. If you are completely unfamiliar with TA, these next examples may be helpful in furthering your understanding and making self-analysis a little easier.

Example One: TA

Leader: Remember how the other day we were asking about moods and how people can be different from one day to the next and I said I would explain that when we met next time? Today, I want to teach a model of human behavior called Transactional Analysis. There are many aspects to this theory and many ways it can be helpful. Today we are just going to cover the three parts of the personality: the Parent, the Adult, and the Child. Each of us has these parts. The Parent part is the bossy or critical part. Also, it is the part that has all kinds of "shoulds." Actually, the Parent has two parts: the critical part and the nurturing part.

John: (*Very critical tone*) This is a bunch of crap!

Leader: (*Calmly*) Thanks, John, for demonstrating the Critical Parent. (*Some laugh.*) John, I'm not trying to embarrass you, but you did just come from the critical parent part of you.

John: All I said was "This is a bunch of crap."

Leader: But you said it in a very critical way—your voice was very critical and your face showed disgust.

John: So, are you saying my voice and face had something to do with what I said?

Leader: Most definitely. When we communicate, we communicate with our words, our voice, and our body language.

Vidal: What's the Child?

Leader: Let me finish the Parent first. Do you understand why I say there are two parts, the critical and the nurturing part?

Hector: Because parents are mean and nice?

Leader: That's on the right track. Let me first clarify something. This is not about parents, like mom and dad, because people who do not have kids have these parts. Let me give you a good example. Last week, we used a lot of Nurturing Parent in helping Jesse deal with the death of his dad. Right, Jesse?

Jesse: That's right. The group really did help me. Thanks.

Leader: So, the Parent part of us can be mean sometimes and very nice sometimes. Think about your Parent part—which is bigger for you?

John: I come across most of the time as critical. My parents are like that too. I didn't get any nurturing ever, unless I was real sick. A couple of times I even faked being sick because my parents would have to pay attention to me instead of doing drugs.
Charlie: I have the nurturing side. I had to with my kids because I had to raise them when their mother was killed. I also have a mean side too, though.

(*For the next ten minutes, the leader gets the members to talk about their Critical Parent and Nurturing Parent.*)

Leader: Let me go to the Child part. There are actually two parts to the Child—the Free Child and the Not OK Child. What do you think the difference is?
Austin: One's out of prison! (*Members laugh.*) I would think the Not OK Child feels bad about himself and the Free Child feels good, plays, and enjoys himself like a kid.
Leader: That's right. The Not OK Child is the part of the person that does not feel good about himself—feels guilty, hurt, angry, jealous, not okay—things like that.
Vidal: I feel all of those at times. Does that mean I am a child?
Leader: No, it just means you sometimes operate from that part. Let me show you a clip from "Friends," a television show which some of you may be familiar with. (*Most nod, indicating they are familiar with "Friends."*) (*The leader plays a three-minute clip that shows two of the main characters in their Critical Parent and Not OK Child, members laugh.*) Now, what part were they in?
Carl: The guy was definitely in his Critical Parent at first, and then was in his Child after she said those things to him.
Jesse: She was hurt and angry and then just busted him. I guess at first she was in her Child and then Critical Parent.

Leader: You're right on the mark. So, can you see that these states are for real? Does the video help some?

John: Yeah. Can we watch more?

Leader: Not now. I want to finish teaching this model. The Adult is the thinking part, or the one that is calm. Like just then, John, you were in your Adult and calmly asked if we could watch more. You could have been in the Critical Parent and asked in a demanding way. Can you ask it that way? (*Members laugh.*)

John: Sure. (*Very demanding voice*) Can we watch more of the show?! (*Everyone laughs.*)

Leader: Exactly right. So, the Adult is the part that listens, thinks, and stays in control. Also, notice that it is not just the words, but also the voice and body language that tell what part a person is in because John said the exact same thing, but used a different voice. Before I go on, any questions or reactions?

Carl: Should one be bigger than the other?

Leader: What do you think?

Tray: All I can say is the associate warden has a huge Critical Parent! That guy doesn't know how to be nice.

Leader: Once you learn this, you can try to figure out what state people are coming from. Back to the question, which part should be the biggest?

Vidal: It would have to be the Adult, but that's sure not true here in the prison. In group, people do pretty good, but not on the unit or in the yard. Can people fight when they are in their Adults?

Leader: (*Looking at the group*)What do you think?

This example shows how a leader can introduce TA and then use it in discussing different situations. The leader would continue talking about the ego states, especially since the members seem to want to know more.

The video clip helped to demonstrate what the leader was talking about and it seemed to get the members interested in learning more. (Once you learn this model, you will easily be able to pick out the different ego states when interacting with others or watching television.)

During the discussion above, the leader could draw various ego states to show what she was talking about. She could have drawn the three parts and the five parts (shown on p. 107). She also could draw unpleasant John with a large Critical Parent and a small Nurturing Parent and small Adult. This would show how he sends messages to the other person's Child ego state. Also, the drawing would show how the other person often ends up in the Not OK Child.

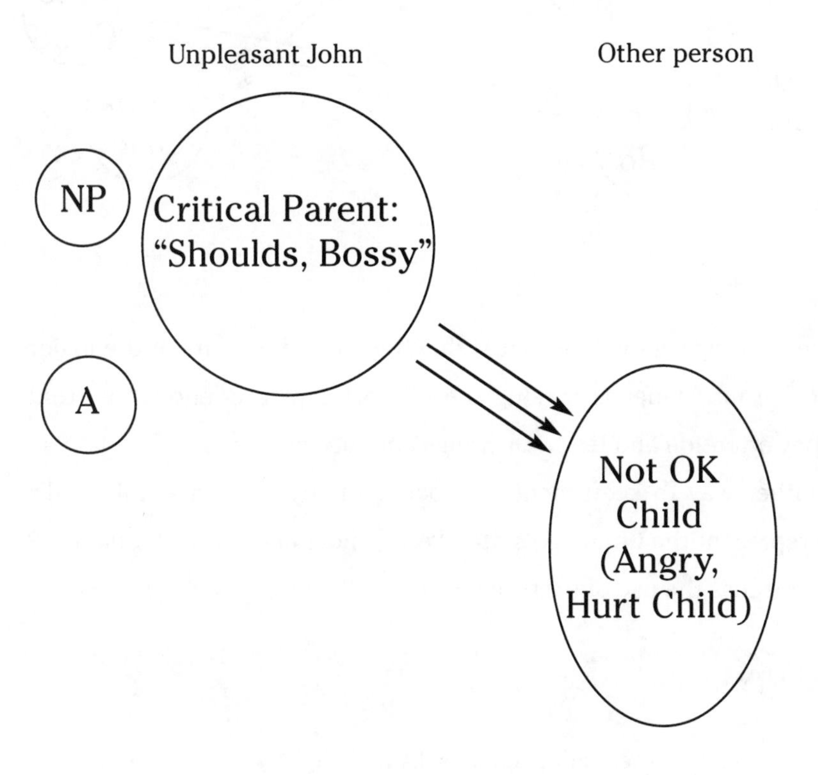

The leader could also draw a pleasant John and show how he could come from his Adult, his Nurturing Parent, and his Free Child.

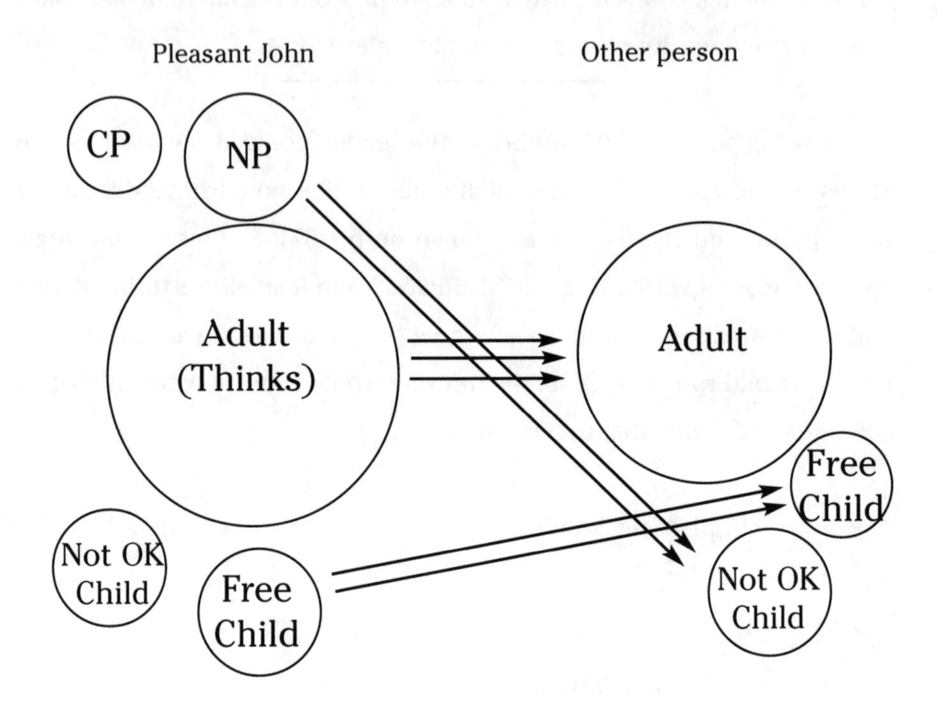

The drawings show how visual this theory can be. One of the major tasks of a group leader is making the group interesting enough so that people pay attention and learn. Drawings add interest.

Another way to keep members focused is by using a small child's chair to represent the Child ego state. We say more about this in Chapter 9 when we discuss the use of props in groups.

Example Two: TA

In this next example, the leader teaches TA in a slightly different way since she is helping the members understand their fighting. The teenagers are currently living in a halfway house.

Kim: My dad and I had a big fight when he came to visit. We always do. I would love to be able to have one peaceful visit with him.

Leader: I can show you something that can help. Actually, this is something all of you can use to understand your interactions with others, especially those interactions that do not go so well. (The leader draws a picture of a fight using the PAC model.)

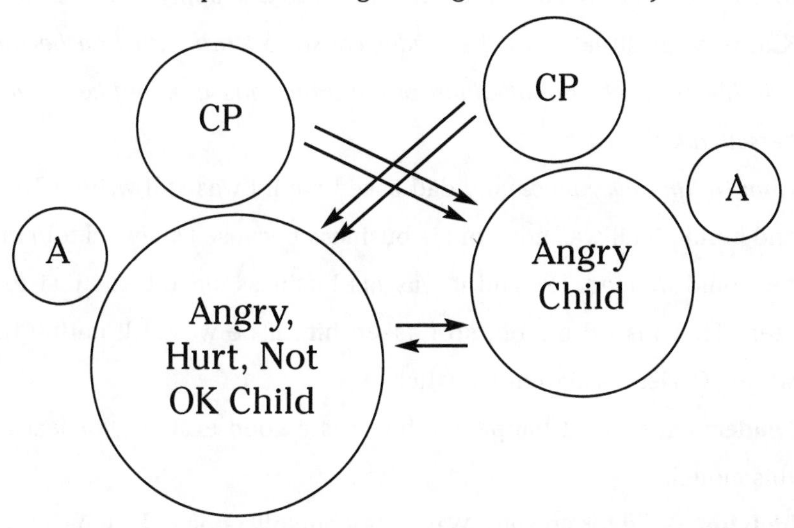

Leader: In each person, there are three parts, the Parent part, the Adult or thinking part, and the Child part. Fights take place when people speak and act from their Parent or Child. Notice how the Adult is sort of on the sidelines, which is true when people fight. If a person stays in her Adult, then she will not really fight with anyone. The Parent part is the bossy part or the "should" part. There is also a Nurturing Parent part, but we are only going to focus on the Critical Parent part. The Adult thinks. For instance, most of you are in your Adult part right now, listening, trying to learn. The Child part is the part that gets angry, hurt, or feels Not OK. The Child also has a Free or OK Child part, but we are only going to focus on the part that is involved in fights. Kim, do you mind if we use this latest fight with your dad as an example?

Erin: I have a fight we can talk about—just happened this morning on my work detail.

Leader: Let's go with Kim's for now, and maybe we will have time to look at yours, Erin. I am sure you will be able to apply what we say to Kim to your situation. (*The leader chose to work with Kim because Erin always seeks the attention of the group and usually likes to hear herself talk.*)

Kim: (*In an angry voice*) My dad asked me if I was still writing Teddy and I told him it was none of his business because I knew if I told him, he would be mad. He said it was his business since I was just fourteen. That pissed me off, so I asked him if he was still dating that whore, Carletta. He went ballistic!

Leader: I'm sorry it happened, but it is a good example for learning this model.

Melvina: Good for you girl. Way to tell him off! I don't like him.

Leader: Hang on. I want you to see that Kim's fight can be understood and can be avoided. Let's start with your dad's question about writing Teddy. What part do you think Kim's dad was in?

Angie: Probably his Parent part. Didn't you say that was the part with "shoulds?" He definitely has "shoulds" for Kim. He does not want Kim to be writing Teddy.

Martha: I agree; otherwise, Kim would not have gone to her Child.

Leader: Good point, and Kim, would you agree, you definitely went to your Child?

Kim: Well, it isn't any of his business!

Erin: (*In a slow, very caring voice*) Kim, you're in your Child right now. We're just trying to help.

Kim: But why doesn't he care about what I want?

Leader: I think he does care. It just doesn't seem like he cares. Could anyone draw the transactions that you think took place between Kim and her dad?

Angie: I'll try. Can we make the circles any size?

Leader: Yes. I hope all of you are thinking about how this applies to you.

Cary: I sure am. Makes sense to me. I feel the same way she does.

Leader: Angie, you give it a try, and we will add to it or help you.

Angie draws the transactions of Kim and her dad. The rest of the group gets involved, including Kim. For the remainder of the session, the leader focuses on how fights occur when people get out of their Adult ego state.

Example Three: TA

This occurs in a later session; the members were taught TA a few weeks before. The leader has continued to use the theory each week in the sessions to analyze situations. This repetition is very important to the process of learning.

Leader: Roy, during the beginning of group, you said you were having a terrible day. Would you like to talk about it?

Roy: I need to. (*In an angry voice*) I'm so mad. I know I am going to get staffed and be in trouble. I got into it with my correctional officer because he would not help me. I told him f@!# off! He told me to get out of his sight. I saw him talking to the supervisor so I know I am going to be in trouble.

Jesse: (*Jokingly*) Get the little chair! (*The leader used a small child's chair a few weeks before to represent the Child ego state.*) Sounds like he's in his Child part.

Roy: This guy has been dragging his feet on contacting my lawyer!

Leader: What state is Roy in now?

Vidal: Not his Adult, and if he stays this way, he'll get in bigger trouble.

Roy: Okay, okay. I am just stewing!

Leader: Roy, we can help. We can use the Parent, Adult, Child model. Do you want us to help?

Roy: Sure. I really don't want to be in trouble.

Leader: I am not sure if we can keep you out of trouble, but this will help for the future. I'll be glad to talk with the supervisor, if it is okay with you. (*To the group*) What does Roy need to do to get to his Adult?

John: First of all, he's got to realize the correctional office has the power, and Roy needs to get in his Adult and play the game. If he stays in his Child, he'll just get himself in more trouble.

Roy: The guy is lazy and incompetent!

Jesse: So what? Does your telling him off change anything other than getting you in trouble?

Roy: (*Thinking for a moment*) I guess not. So, my Adult has to understand this.

Leader: Remember how last week I said over and over again, "The Adult has his expectations in line with reality?"

Carl: You sure don't have your expectations in line with reality about the correctional officer. I deal with him a lot and I just accept that he's lazy. I just keep on him, and eventually he usually will do what I ask. I used to go to my Child, but learning this stuff helped me to see how silly I was being. That one time during group when I had to sit in the little chair really stuck with me.

John: I have not had an angry outburst since the time I learned this. I start to get mad and then say to myself, "John, get in your Adult." It helps me.

In this example, the members understand TA and are using it to help another member and seem to be using it in their daily lives. This discussion of TA is brief and is only meant to provide an overview of the theory and its usefulness. For additional information on TA, we suggest you go to the web site *www.ta-tutor.com.* Some wonderful, creative information on TA is available at this site.

Reality Therapy

William Glasser developed his theory called Reality Therapy in the mid 1960s. Glasser, in his book *Reality Therapy* (1965), discussed a program that he set up for young women committed to an institution in California. Later, Glasser made some modifications to the theory and changed its name to Choice Theory (Glasser, 1998). Much work has been done in prisons using Reality Therapy. Cohen and Sordo (1984) presented in their article many different ways that Reality Therapy could be used with adult offenders. In his book, Wubbolding (2000) discusses the basic needs of people that Glasser spelled out in his first book on Reality Therapy:

- Survival/self-preservation
- Belonging
- Power
- Freedom or independence
- Fun or enjoyment

These basic needs are compromised when in prison. Group leaders can use this theory to help inmates understand their needs and their behavior centering around each of these needs. Often inmates do not understand the motivation behind the crimes they committed nor do they understand why they act certain ways in prison. This theory goes a long way to help explain behaviors that led to incarceration and behaviors that lead to problems in prison. Getting members to understand their basic needs and how these needs drive their behavior is very helpful to inmates.

One of the major techniques of Reality Therapy that is excellent for corrections counseling focuses on getting inmates to answer these questions:

- "What do you want?"
- "What are you currently doing?"
- "Is what you're doing going to get you what you want?"
- "What is your plan?"

These questions get members to focus on the reality of their behavior. This is very valuable for a prison population since the purpose of many of the groups in prisons is to get members to change what they are doing because if they do not, they will end up back in prison. We strongly encourage all correctional workers to become familiar with the basics of Reality Therapy.

Example: Reality Therapy

Leader: Rubin, let me ask you this, "What do you want?" In fact, each of you can think about how you would answer the question, "What do you want?"

Rubin: I want to get out of this place as soon as possible and never come back here. I hate it here!

Leader: Is what you're doing going to get you what you want?

Omar: I want to be home by next Christmas. I am . . . .

Leader: (*Knowing that Omar always tries to get the group to focus on him, the leader interrupts*) Omar, I want us to focus on Rubin right now and then we will focus on others. Rubin, is what you're doing going to get you what you want?

Rubin: You mean blowing off the classes and messing up on my work detail?

Leader: Yeah, those things and threatening Luke in the lunchroom. Will that get you out of here as soon as possible?

Rubin: No.

Leader: Each of you think about if what you are doing is going to get you what you want. Actually, did anyone answer that question with an answer like "go to college," "have a job I like," "get married," or "have children?"

Michael: I did. I want to become a counselor and work with troubled kids like us.

Ernest: I want to find a good job, maybe as a chef. That's why I like my work detail in the kitchen. I think it will get me started when I get out of here.

Omar: All I think about is getting home.

Leader: I guess I want all of you to want to get out of here and to stay out. Now, Rubin, if what you are doing is not working, here's the question, what is your plan to get you what you want?

Rubin: Huh?

Leader: You told us what you want, and what you are doing is not going to get you what you want, so you are going to have to have a plan for getting what you want or it will not happen. Like Ernest, he's got a plan, or Michael, he's got a plan. Both of them are working hard in school here, doing extra things, reading, and they stay out of trouble because they know that getting into trouble does not get them what they want.

Rubin: How do I get a plan?

Ernest: You have to get your goal in mind and then do not do anything that detracts from that goal.

Leader: Would you like to focus on a plan that will get you what you want?

Rubin: Yes.

Leader: Let's look at a plan that will get you out of here and keep you out. (*Leader writes "Rubin's Plan" on the board.*) I want each of you to think about what Rubin needs to have in his plan in order to get out of here and stay out of here. Also, please think about this for yourself as well. Do you have a plan that will get you what you want in your life?

In this example, the leader is using the ideas from Reality Therapy to help the members look at the reality of life, which is that they need a plan to get what they want, and often what they are doing is not going to get them what they want. An excellent current book on Reality Therapy is *Reality Therapy for the 21st Century* by Robert Wubbolding (2000).

Psychodrama

Psychodrama is a form of group counseling that was developed for group work by J. L. Moreno (1964) back in the 1930s. The client is given a chance to act out and thereby experience various aspects of his or her life situation in front of an audience. Psychodrama differs from role-playing in that the leader follows specific guidelines for how the "drama" should unfold. Also there are techniques that the leader uses to try to get the working member deeper into his or her feelings (Van Voorhis, Braswell, and Lester, 2000). Because special training is needed for a therapist to conduct psychodrama, we only mention it here and encourage you to explore psychodrama further once you feel you have mastered the skills in this book. When psychodrama is conducted well, very deep and painful emotions are usually generated.

Haskell (1960) reviewed the uses of psychodrama in prisons up to 1960. Miller (1960) did some very interesting interventions with teenagers using psychodrama in which he had judges and probation officers watch the psychodrama sessions to gain a better understanding of the family life of the delinquent teenager. Other more recent studies have also shown psychodrama to be effective with offenders (Gaudin and Kurtz, 1985; Schrumski, Feldman, Harvey, and Holiman, 1984).

Other Theories

A number of other helpful theories can be applied to groups within a correctional setting, but we wanted to focus on the three that we find are particularly useful. Since this book is about group leading and not about theories, we felt that a brief overview would be sufficient. Those who do not feel strong in theory may want to do additional reading or attend workshops that focus on the specific theories that interest them.

Concluding Comments

Knowing and using theories on how people feel, think, and behave is what makes treatment group leaders capable of effecting change in their members. Entire books are written on each of these theories and on many other theories. This chapter showed how helpful theories can be for a group leader. A solid knowledge of at least one counseling theory is necessary for success as a treatment group leader. The use of a theory-based approach throughout the sessions adds a dimension to groups that takes the members far beyond just airing their thoughts and feelings. Rational Emotive Behavioral Therapy is based on the idea that thoughts cause feelings and can be explained using an ABC model. Transactional Analysis is an excellent theory for showing how people interact. Using drawings and chairs, including a small child's chair to represent the different ego states, can help to depict different parts of the person. Reality Therapy is an excellent theory for getting members to focus on what they want, what they are doing, and to develop a plan for getting what they want. Psychodrama is a form of group therapy that can generate powerful emotions and requires additional training in the specific techniques unique to it.

Exercises

An exercise is any activity conducted by the leader that engages the members in some way. Exercises should be used in almost all kinds of groups and are used for many different reasons. They are used to warm up the members, to gather information, to get members focused, or to get members engaged and thinking. In this chapter we discuss how to choose, introduce, conduct, and process exercises. In the next two chapters, we discuss many different kinds of exercises.

Choosing the Exercise

The use of exercises requires many skills from the group leader. The first skill is the ability to pick the right exercise for the group. The most important consideration when picking an exercise is its purpose—that is, is the exercise for warm-up, focusing, or serious exploration? Also, will the exercise lead to discussion relevant to what the leader plans to discuss during the session? The purpose, in part, will dictate what exercise the leader chooses. Far too often, leaders use exercises that are either not on the topic planned for the day or not even related to the overall purpose of the group. They pick the exercise because they liked it when they did it or when they read about it in a book. Exercises can help the group to focus on a topic or they can distract the group from the topic. The key is to pick wisely. Since each group is different, some exercises that work well with some groups absolutely bomb with other groups.

When picking an exercise, always answer the following questions:

- Is it relevant for this group?
- Does it fit with the topic to be discussed?
- Will it work well given the age, maturity, and mental capacities of the members?
- Will it be interesting for members?
- What benefit will it have?

Often leaders just pick an exercise because it is related to the subject they want to cover without thinking how this exercise will be used to help the members. If the leader chooses exercises that are not relevant, the members may see the exercises as just "passing time." This is not the tone that leaders want for their groups since, in general, too often inmates are only interested in "passing time."

Along with the exercise being relevant, a leader always has to consider if it will be interesting for the members. Often, some exercises are relevant, but the members may not find them interesting. It is the responsibility of the group leader to pick exercises that are interesting. Also, using exercises that interest the members makes leading much easier. As you gain experience, you will learn what exercises tend to be interesting for a given population.

One important thing to consider is how much time the exercise takes. Many leaders make the mistake of using exercises that take too much time, thus not allowing time for processing. For groups that meet for two or three hours, leaders can use longer exercises, but there should always be enough time to discuss the exercise and not have the exercise take up the majority of the time. One example of this is the use of movies or videotapes. Leaders should rarely let the movie or tape take up the entire time because the purpose of the movie is to generate thought and discussion. For some movies, it is helpful to tell the members certain things to look for while watching them. Then, afterwards, there can be a discussion on these points as well as others. For longer movies or videos, the leaders should divide the movie into parts, showing one part during each contact with the group. This allows time for discussion and processing of the information.

As we have mentioned, trust is a very big issue in correctional settings. One consideration when using exercises is, how much does this exercise involve trust among the members? If it does, is there enough trust in the group? Many deepening exercises are designed with the assumption that there is trust in the group. If there is little trust, deepening exercises will go nowhere or may even cause harm. An example of this would be where members are giving each other feedback. If the trust is low, members will not say much, not volunteer to be the recipient of feedback, give superficial feedback, or give very strong negative feedback. Feedback exercises may even "backfire" and compromise the level of trust already attained.

Introducing the Exercise

Leaders always should pay attention to how they introduce an exercise since the introduction sets the tone for the exercise. Beginning leaders often do not pay attention to how they introduce an exercise. An energetic voice tone where the leader shows enthusiasm for the exercise helps to get members into a learning mode. A serious voice tone can be very useful in getting members ready to do a more serious exercise where members are going to be thoughtful and introspective.

A common mistake when introducing an exercise is to first give the members a handout of some kind and then start giving instructions. What happens in a case like this is the members start reading or looking at the handout and do not pay attention to the instructions. Giving instructions before handing out the materials ensures that the members will pay attention to the directions. Another common mistake is to give all the directions at once, such as "Pair up, decide who is going first, get out a sheet of paper and something to write with, sit with backs to each other, and tell a positive story from childhood." These instructions would be better given in small steps, like "pair up" (give them time to do this), "decide who is going to go first," and so forth. When you give all the instructions at one time, invariably someone will miss some part and you have to repeat them again. Taking the directions one step at a time is particularly important in groups with slow learners or those with mental problems.

Another mistake that leaders make during the introduction of an exercise is to use a nonserious or "light" tone, which gives the impression that the exercise is to be something fun and not serious. If it is a serious exercise, you will want to use an inviting, serious voice pattern that sets an appropriate tone.

Conducting the Exercise

With many exercises, the leader has to pay attention throughout an exercise to ensure that the exercise has the desired effect. For instance, with written exercises, the leader will want to make sure that the members are able to write and then make sure they are doing the task instead of something else. For reading exercises, it is very important to make sure the members can read or that they will not be too embarrassed to admit that they cannot. In cases where a member cannot read or the leader is not sure if a member can read, the leader or another member can read the instructions or the common reading to the whole group. With movement or physical exercises, some members may not be able to participate and the leader should plan for this ahead of time so that the members are not embarrassed.

Many exercises require time to think; yet, some members will want to talk during this time. The leader needs to make sure this does not happen. This especially happens when members are writing or reading something and they get done ahead of the others, so they start to talk. If the leader allows for "chatting" while others are working, the working members may become quite frustrated or distracted. Leaders not only have the right but are only doing their job well when they keep the members quiet during these times.

One problem that can come up during the conducting of an exercise is that members do not stay focused on the exercise. This happens especially when members are asked to pair up or get in small groups and talk about a topic, issue, or feeling. Often they start talking about other things or start joking with each other. What also happens when members get in small groups is one person will dominate the conversation and thus the others do not get to share their ideas or feelings. The leader should try, whenever possible, to keep the members on task and make sure that each person gets a turn to talk. This can be done by going from one dyad or group to another and briefly listening to the conversation to see that they are doing what they were asked to do. When they are not, the leader needs to step in and remind them of the task.

With some exercises, the members will have a certain amount of time to complete a task. The leader should give time warnings, such as "You have two more minutes" or "Thirty more seconds." With some movement exercises, members may tend to laugh and joke around even though the leader is trying to conduct a serious exercise. When this occurs, the leader needs to say in a serious voice something like, "Please, no laughter. Give each member a chance to have her experience."

With certain exercises, there will be times when members will not want to participate. They may not want to share for any of a number of possible reasons:

- They may lack trust in the group.
- They may fear looking foolish.
- They may not want to be a part of the group.
- They may want to be rebellious.
- They may be trying to sabotage the group.

Leaders must anticipate members not wanting to participate and have a plan for dealing with it. Often, letting the member sit out is fine. Sometimes, leaders have the member leave, but frequently this is not possible nor the best strategy because often the nonparticipating member gains by listening and watching.

In exercises where members are working in pairs, if there are two or more nonparticipants, whenever possible, pair the two together. By not pairing them with members who want to participate, this at least prevents the nonparticipants from disrupting others who want to participate. The leader may direct them to do another activity that may be of interest or have them just observe what the others are doing. The key is to not let one or two members who do not want to participate throw off the entire exercise.

Often we are asked whether you should force members to participate. In most cases, it is best not to force members to participate because that can create many different problems. Usually not much is gained by forcing inmates to be in an exercise, although there are times when some forcing may be appropriate. Sometimes pushing members to give or receive feedback, state something in a round exercise, or answer a sentence completion can be valuable. By getting the members to participate, they get involved in a more active way rather than "sitting on the sidelines." Leaders should be very careful if they are going to make someone do something that they have said they do not want to do. This is not only counterproductive but can be ultimately dangerous in a setting with an impulsive, potentially violent population.

Processing the Exercise

Most effective exercises are conducted for two purposes: generating reactions, thoughts, and feelings and generating discussion. The discussion of the different reactions, thoughts, and feelings is what we call "processing" and is the most important part of an exercise. Unfortunately, many leaders do not understand this and end up using exercises to fill up time. Skilled leaders anticipate what reactions are going to occur as a result of conducting an exercise and plan how they are going to process the exercise so that the time spent doing the exercise was worthwhile and beneficial to the members. Skilled leaders think of good questions, rounds, or other follow-up activities that may be used so that members have a chance to share their thoughts, feelings, and reactions. Experienced leaders always know how they are going to process an exercise before they conduct it, even though they never know exactly where the processing will take them since exercises generate many different reactions (Kees and Jacobs, 1990).

Some leaders think that no processing is necessary. Untrained leaders either conduct exercises that take up the entire session or conduct one exercise after another. Both of these mistakes allow very little time to process the exercise. It is important to remember that the purpose of the exercise is to stimulate members to think and react and then have them share their thoughts and reactions at a meaningful level. Two other common mistakes in processing include letting the members go off on tangents and not spending enough time processing. Often leaders get members to share initial reactions but do not spend extra time to go deeper into the thoughts and feelings that were generated. The best way to go to a deeper, more meaningful level during the processing phase of an exercise is to prepare ahead of time thought-provoking, usually theory-based questions to ask during the processing. Below are examples of bad and good processing.

Example One: Bad Processing

Members were asked to make a list of unfinished psychological business in their lives and now the leader is having them share their lists. Four have already shared.

> **Olen:** My list is not too long: my mom, for leaving us with dad, my dad, for doing drugs and leaving us all the time, and my girlfriend, who cheated on me.

Randy: I'd say my brother, who turned me in, and my girlfriend, who broke up with me because I went to prison.

Leader: Sam, you're the last one.

Sam: Mom and dad, grandmother, and Mrs. Smith, my third-grade teacher. She made my life hell.

Leader: Was it interesting to make the list?

Randy: It was for me. I could feel myself getting angry as I thought about it. My brother came to see me once and I would not even talk to him.

Sam: I have not thought about Mrs. Smith for a long time. She really was mean to me, and I think she is the reason why I was turned off to school.

Norm: I got turned off in school because I was a terrible reader and people made fun of me.

Leader: Other thoughts or feelings?

Olen: I kind of liked school. It got me away from home. I enjoyed math and reading.

Randy: I like math and reading, too.

Leader: How were others of you in math and reading?

In this example, the leader went with the flow of the conversation rather than directing the processing of the exercise to more meaningful discussion.

Example One: Good Processing

Members were asked to make a list of unfinished psychological business in their lives and now the leader is having them share their lists. Four have already shared.

Randy: I'd say my brother, who turned me in, and my girlfriend, who broke up with me because I went to prison.

Leader: Sam, you're the last one.

Sam: Mom and dad, grandmother, and Mrs. Smith, my third grade teacher. She made my life hell.

Leader: (*Wanting to deepen the focus using the ideas just shared*) The reason I had you look at this is because unresolved anger carries over into your life today. How does your anger when you were young affect you today?

Norm: Are you saying that a lot of what we feel today is a result of what we felt growing up?

Leader: Yes, that is definitely what I am talking about. Looking at past, unresolved anger can help you understand the anger you feel today.

Randy: I think I am mad all the time because of them.

Leader: Exactly. Would you like to work on your anger, Randy?

Randy: I think it would be helpful.

Leader: How about others of you—do you want to finish some unfinished business with anger?

Olen: I think it would help me to look at my anger at my mom and dad—that's a big thing for me.

Leader: Okay, let's do that. (*The group spends the rest of the time focusing on dealing with the anger issues that were on their lists.*)

The leader made sure the processing of their list of unfinished business led to meaningful discussion about working on how to get rid of some of the anger that the members still had.

Example Two: Bad Processing

After asking members of a sex offenders group to imagine apologizing for what they did, the leader starts to process the exercise.

Leader: What was it like to imagine doing that?

Sandy: I think for the first time I could see it from her perspective.

Rajul: I am still thinking.

Steve: I couldn't get over being mad at Janie for putting me in this place! She's so two-faced. She acts so goody-goody in court and all and when she was around me she was a little flirt. Heck, even though she is ten, she knew what she was doing. When you asked us to imagine what the scene would be, Janie's mom came in my mind and I spent my time imagining talking to her. I am really pissed off at her because she would work evenings and leave me to take care of Janie. It was her daughter, damn it!

Leader: So, Steve, you have a lot of anger still. How about others?

Vinny: I couldn't get into it either because I kept thinking about what that girl said at the trial and how my lawyer didn't do anything. I know I could have done a better job than that idiot I had. Someone said there are law books in the library here. How do I find them?

Steve: You ask the officer in charge. They have them behind the desk. Some of them are hard to understand.

Sandy: Josh, in Unit A, is great at helping with lawyer stuff. I think he went to law school for a couple of years before he got busted.

Steve: I think he only went one year. I'll tell you who else is good. Big John. He understands all that stuff. Heck, maybe I can help you. What legal questions did you have?

The leader did not focus the group so no productive processing took place.

Example Two: Good Processing

After asking members of a sex offenders group to imagine apologizing for what they did, the leader starts to process the exercise.

Leader: What was it like to imagine doing that?
Sandy: I think for the first time I could see it from her perspective.
Rajul: I am still thinking.
Steve: I couldn't get over being mad at Janie for putting me in this place! She's so two-faced. She acts so goody-goody in court and all and when she was around me she was a little flirt. Heck, even though she is ten, she knew what she was doing. When you asked us to imagine what the scene would be, Janie's mom came in my mind. I spent my time imagining talking to her. I am really pissed off at her because she would work evenings and leave me to take care of Janie. It was her daughter, damn it!
Leader: Did others of you have an experience like Sandy did—seeing it from her perspective?
Albert: I did.
Bryce: It got me to thinking.
Leader: Good. That's why we did the exercise. One of the purposes of the group is to get you to look at what you did and how that makes others feel.
Sandy: I'd like to talk about what I saw. It was powerful. I have some questions.
Leader: Go ahead.

The leader focused on the purpose of the exercise, which was to get the members to think about the other person's feelings. The leader saw that Sandy had gotten into the exercise and decided to hold the focus on him, knowing that Sandy's work would help others as well. He also made sure members did not follow up on Steve's comment.

In these examples, we emphasized the importance of processing an exercise. It is the processing part of the exercise that usually leads to deeper discussion, which, in turn, leads to the group being meaningful. A leader should always have some idea of how she is going to process an exercise before she ever uses the exercise in her group. That way, during the processing, the leader can direct the discussion to relevant and beneficial topics.

Concluding Comments

Exercises are essential for most groups in correctional settings because usually the members are not going to bring much material to the groups. The four aspects of using an exercise include: picking the right one, introducing it properly, conducting it, and processing it effectively. By far, the most important part is the processing in that it is the processing of exercises that makes them a valuable tool for helping inmates gain insight and knowledge.

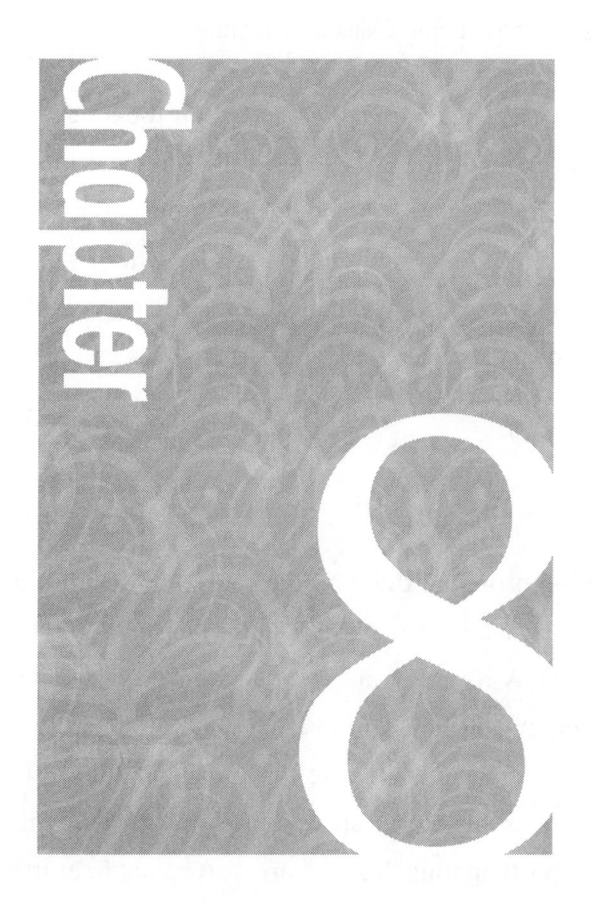

Types of Exercises

In this chapter, we discuss different types of exercises from which leaders can choose. Some of the exercises involve sharing, writing, moving, working together, working alone, or just watching. We give examples of each of the exercises and we offer sample dialogs that start where the exercise is being introduced. Our main purpose is to provide an idea of how the exercise can be used, so we use fewer members than most leaders probably will have in their groups. In this chapter, we discuss a number of exercises, but we encourage you to search out group books and information related to the specific population with which you are working. Many books and workbooks exist that provide exercises. However, some of the material may have exercises that are either too long, too complicated, or not meaningful enough. Just because an exercise is in a book or you experienced it at an in-service training does not mean it is a good exercise for a particular group. Always carefully consider whether the exercise is right for particular groups. As you gain more experience, you will be able to make up your own exercises for some of the issues you plan to cover in your groups.

Rounds

The round is probably the most versatile and helpful exercise that leaders can use to make their groups more interesting (Jacobs, Masson, and Harvill, 2002). A round is an exercise where the leader goes from member to member and hears from each member, usually with a brief answer. Rounds are valuable because they get members to talk. Most of the time, members are willing to share a brief answer when they see that everyone else is participating. Rounds are also valuable in that they limit how much each person talks. This makes stopping long-winded members easier because the activity calls for short answers. Rounds are useful in large groups that often exist in prison settings because they allow each member to contribute something in an efficient way. Many rounds call for a word, number, or phrase. Number rounds include such things as the rating of the amount of anger, guilt, or fear on a scale of 1-to-10 with 1 being very low and 10 being very high. Other 1-to-10 rounds could be as follows:

- On a scale of 1-to-10, how was your week?
- On a scale of 1-to-10, how much did you like the videotape that was shown?
- How much trust do you feel in the group on a scale of 1-to-10 with 10 being lots of trust?

Word rounds include "yes/no" rounds such as "Do you have anything you want to talk about today?" or "Yes or No regarding if you want to talk about _______[the leader inserts the topic that was planned for the day]." This round helps the leader to quickly gauge the interest in a topic. If there is not much interest in the topic, the leader should have planned other topics that can be pursued.

Word or phrase rounds get members to share briefly about something. Examples would be the following:

- In a word or phrase, how would you describe your day?
- In a word or phrase, what is the hardest thing about being in prison?
- In a word or phrase, what is one thing that stood out about the reading?
- In a word or phrase, what did you learn from group today?

A variation of the word or phrase round is to ask for a sentence or two about some topic. The advantage of using the number, word, phrase, or comment round is that the leader can hear from everyone. Also, the round keeps one person from dominating since the members are being asked for just a brief response.

Example One: Round

Leader: Let's do a round of how the week has been. A 1 indicates that is it has been terrible, and a 10 shows that it has been great. Who wants to start?

Amy: 8

Andrea: 7

Cheryl: 4

Nina: 3

Patty: 10

Tina: 8

Dottie: 9

Leader: Most had a good week. Cheryl, do you or Nina want to comment on your week? (*Both nod yes.*) Cheryl, why don't you go first?

Cheryl: My boyfriend was supposed to visit and he didn't, and I have not heard from him.

Leader: Would you like to talk about that?

Cheryl: Yes.

Leader: Okay. Let's first hear from Nina about why her week was not good.

Nina: I got in trouble at work for smoking.

In this example, the round helped the leader to learn very quickly how members felt about the previous week. Also, the leader learned that Nina and Cheryl have issues they want to try to resolve.

Example Two: Round

Leader: We're going to focus on guilt and shame today. First, I want to do a quick round. Using a word or phrase, what comes to your mind when I say the words, "guilt" and "shame?"

Linda: What I did to my kids.

Anita: My uncle and what he did to me.

Rose: All the people I stole from.

Sara: Why I didn't quit using while I was pregnant. I ruined my child (*Starts crying*).

Leader: (*Looking at Sara, and with a warm voice*) Let me get Holly's comment, then, Sara, we'll come back to you.

Holly: I used to feel all kinds of guilt but one counselor I had really helped me. I don't feel very much guilt now.

Leader: Holly, that's good. Hopefully you can share some of what your counselor taught you. Sara, do you want to talk about your pain?

The round served as a good way for the leader to find out how the members relate to the topic. Also, by conducting the round, the members got focused on the topic and more than likely the leader would be able to help Sara and others go to a deeper level.

A variation of the round and something that has a similar effect is to have the members do nonverbal things such as putting their thumbs up or down or using their fingers to indicate their 1-to-10 rating about something. The value is the same—members are offering their opinion about some issue or concept.

Written Exercises

Written exercises are very useful in getting members focused. They also help in drawing out individuals. Written exercises include sentence completions, lists, circling ratings on a 1-to-7 scale, or any other activity that has the members writing. The benefit of written exercises is that members get focused when having to put on paper their answers or thoughts. Also, it is easier to draw out members when they already have answers in front of them. That is, members usually do not feel on the spot when asked to read what they wrote. In any group, the leader should make sure that the members can read and write if they are asked to fill out a sentence completion or write a list. Also, if the leader asks inmates to write for any length of time, she should not wait until the last person is finished if it looks like that person is going to need a lot more time than the other members. By waiting too long, the leader loses the attention of the group. Below we discuss a number of useful written exercises.

Sentence Completion

The sentence completion is an excellent exercise to use to get discussion started. Members usually get focused when filling out the sentences and are curious about what others said. Usually it is best to have no more than five sentences. Sometimes one sentence is enough to discuss for an entire group. When developing a sentence completion form, the leader should make sure the sentences are relevant to what he wants to discuss in the group. Below are a number of possible incomplete sentences. A leader would not want to put all these on the same form because they are about various topics. These are examples of the types of sentences that leaders can use in their groups.

One thing I like about group is______________________________.

One thing I don't like about group is__________________________.

The thing I fear most about being in jail is______________________.

The hardest thing about my first week here has been

____.

When I think of my mom, I feel ______________________________.

When I get out, my biggest fear is ___________________________.

My greatest strength is ____.

My greatest regret is____.

As I see it, the most difficult thing about our task is

____.

Something that stands out to me about last week is

____.

The skilled leader will use the sentences to get members to share and then will pick up on their answers and try to engage the members in meaningful discussion centered around their answers.

Ratings

Another excellent exercise for getting members focused on a topic is to develop a rating form that has a 1-to-5 or a 1-to-7 scale. Members circle the number that best represents how they feel. Often leaders will make up a three-to-five question rating form on the subject they plan to talk about in the group. An example would be the following:

I regret my involvement in drugs.

strongly disagree	disagree	neutral	agree	strongly agree
1	2	3	4	5

My friends and associates have a lot to do with whether I will relapse.

strongly disagree	disagree	neutral	agree	strongly agree
1	2	3	4	5

Drugs are not a problem for me.

strongly disagree	disagree	neutral	agree	strongly agree
1	2	3	4	5

By having members first circle their answers, the leader can ask for what they circled and then generate discussion from their answers.

Egogram

One written exercise that gets members to think about their personality is drawing an egogram. The egogram comes out of Transactional Analysis theory. It is a bar graph of the seven ego states: Critical Parent of others, Critical Parent of self, Nurturing Parent of others, Nurturing Parent of self, the Adult, the Free or OK Child, and the Not OK Child. The leader explains the different egostates and then has the members draw their egogram as they see themselves in the institution and/or how they see themselves away from the institution if that is relevant. The egogram serves as a good introduction to TA and also can be done at different times during the group meetings to see if, in fact, people are changing. An egogram might look something like the one below.

Egograms: Critical Parent (CP) (Self/Others), Nurturing Parent (NP) (Self/Others), Adult, Free Child, Not OK Child

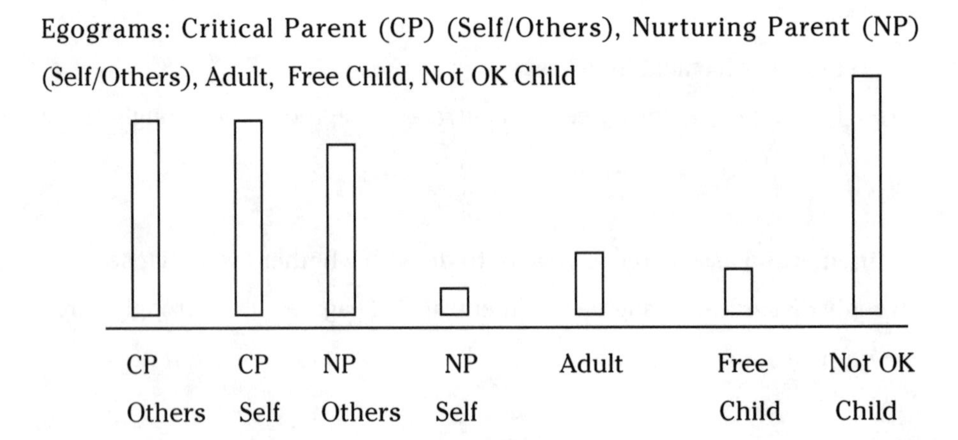

Drawing an egogram is an excellent activity for getting members to investigate the different parts of their personalities. It gives members a chance to see what ego states need to come down and which ones need to go up. The egogram can stimulate discussion that can last a couple of sessions if the leader chooses to have each person discuss in detail their egogram and their feelings about it.

Example: Egogram

Leader: Remember how last week we talked about the different parts of our personality and we talked about the Parent, Adult, and Child parts? Today, we are going to do an exercise. Each of you will need a piece of paper and pencil. You are going to draw what is called an egogram, which is a bar graph of not three but seven ego states. When we are done, we will discuss your reaction to your egogram. Most people find this quite interesting. We will do this again in a couple of months and see if you are changing. Let's start with the first ego state, Critical Parent of Others. Draw how much you see yourself as critical of others. I'm drawing an example of someone who is high on Critical Parent of Others. Everyone understand what I mean by critical parent of others? Archie Bunker, if you know that guy from television, had a large critical parent of others.

Leader: (*Allowing a few seconds for them to draw*) Okay, now the next one is Critical Parent of Self. This would be high if you always beat up on yourself. I know many of you do this, so yours would be high. Everyone understand this one?

Leader: (*Allowing a few seconds for them to draw*) The third one is Nurturing Parent of Others. How nurturing are you of others? Some of you are and some of you are not.

Leader: (*Allowing a few seconds for them to draw*) This next ego state is important because many of you do not nurture yourself. This one is Nurturing Parent of Self. Do you nurture yourself, or do you count on others to do it for you? I am drawing this one low because many people in prison do not know how to nurture themselves.

Leader: (*Allowing a few seconds for them to draw*) The next ego state is the Adult. This is the thinking part, the rational part.

Leader: (*Allowing a few seconds for them to draw*) This ego state is the Fun or Free Child part—the part that likes to have fun. Let's say you draw this without the use of drugs. Do you know how to have fun when no drugs are included?

Leader: (*Allowing a few seconds for them to draw*) The last part is the Not OK Child or the Guilty Child or the Angry Child. This is the part that feels negative about things, maybe from earlier experiences, maybe from being here. This one is usually large for people in prison.

Leader: (*Allowing a few seconds for them to draw*) Now, take a few moments and look at what you drew. Think about it. Do you see parts you want to change?

Leader: (*Allowing a few seconds for them to think*) Any comments?

Vidal: I don't like what I see. The Adult part is towered over by the Not OK part and my Free Child is not big at all.

Richard: I have a very large Critical Parent.

Otto: Of yourself or others? Mine is very big of myself.

Vidal: Of both. I am critical of everyone and myself. (*Members laugh because he is very critical in group.*)

Leader: This is why we do this exercise—to get you to see your parts of your personality. Let's hear from others, and then we'll take a look at ways you can change your egogram.

Stroke Economy

Leaders can use the stroke economy exercise to get members to think about the positive and negative people with whom they interact on a regular basis. In this exercise, the leader has members list the initials or first names of people the members interact with regularly. Then, the members are asked to indicate if the person is positive or negative in their lives. The members are asked to put pluses (+) or minuses (-) beside each person's name on their list. They can use one, two, or three pluses or minuses to indicate the amount of positive or negative feelings they have about their interaction with that person. They may even give a person a plus and a minus. When the members are finished doing this, they are asked to comment on "their stroke economy." By doing the exercise and processing it, members get a chance to see interaction patterns and see how some may have a "poor economy." Some realize that very few positive people are in their lives.

Example: Stroke Economy

This is a group of teenagers who are on probation. Their probation officer has them come to group meetings once every two weeks for two hours. It is about one hour into the meeting.

Leader: The reason for the paper and pencil is that I am going to do an exercise called Stroke Economy. On the sheet of paper I want you to list the first names of people you interact with on a regular basis, maybe every day or once a week or once a month.

Sharon: Are these people we like?

Leader: It is people you regularly are around or talk to. You may like them or not like them. (*Leader allows about two minutes for people to* *think about their list.*) Okay, now beside each name put a + or a double + or even triple + if they are very positive and put a - or double - or triple - if they are negative or you may even put a + and - for the same person.

Leader: (*After two or three minutes*) What do you think of your stroke economy?

Gloria: Mine stinks. I don't have many pluses. My sister is a triple + but she is in college now so I don't see her very much. And my old boyfriend—we e-mail a lot because he lives in Canada now. I have lots of minuses—my mom, my stepdad, lots of girls at school.

Leader: Can you see why you feel down a lot? (*Gloria nods.*) This is an important part of having a positive attitude—being around positive people. Actually, I hope many of you can see that your economy needs to improve, just like in our country now; people are working hard to fix the poor economy.

Heather: My economy is strange. I have some great positive people and some great negative people, and the big one for me is my boyfriend. I gave him one plus and two minuses. The people I ride to school with used to be positive but they are mostly minuses now, especially since I got in trouble and don't want to do the things they are into.

Leader: Heather, do you see ways to fix your economy?

Heather: I think so.

Leader: We'll come back to you. First, let's hear from Lorraine and Donna, and then we'll spend the rest of the time talking about ways to change our stroke economies. How does that sound? (*All nod or say "good."*)

In this exercise, he leader asked a deepening-type question when she asked Heather if she saw ways to fix her stroke economy. (Leaders should always be thinking of deepening-type questions that may relate to an exercise.) This question was meant to get Heather and other members to start thinking more deeply about changing people in their lives. The leader would continue discussing the members' stroke economies and changes they could make, such as getting rid of some of the negative people or at least spending less time with them and more time with positive people. The leader also would discuss ways of getting more positive strokes from people and activities.

Board of Directors

The board of directors exercise is excellent for getting members to look at whom they turn to when making decisions. The leader has the members quickly draw a picture of a rectangle with ten circles around it to look like a table with chairs around it.

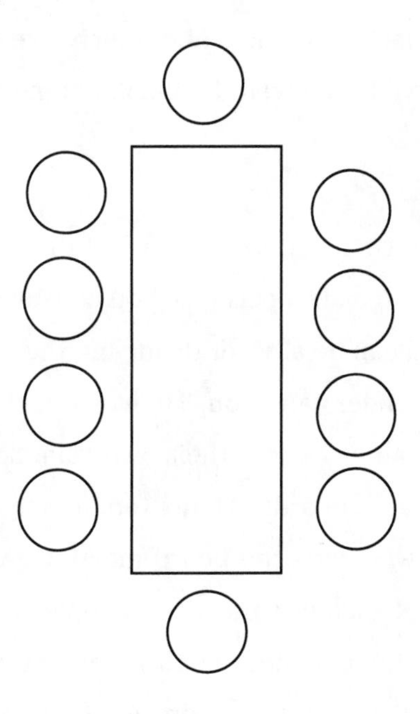

The leader would give the members a few minutes to fill in their board of directors—their internal decision makers—and then would ask for comments and reactions. Often inmates see that their board is very small or that they have people on the board who are not tuned in to who they are. If the members do not bring up the chairperson, the leader does. Many have themselves as the chairperson, which may or may not be a good thing. Some who have someone else as chair realize that their chairperson is bad for them. Many times members see that they need to "fire" some people from their board if they want to live a better life. The exercise is valuable because if the members do not change their boards, they will be influenced by people who will lead them back to a life of crime and/or drug use.

Example: Board of Directors

Members are all on home arrest and have to come to group meetings once a week. This is the third meeting and it is about forty-five minutes into the session. The members have been given the blank outline of their board of directors.

> **Leader:** All of you have an internal board of directors inside your head. When you have to make decisions, you consult your board. The people on your board can be alive or dead, and they may understand you or they may not understand you. They can have your best interest at heart or they can be out for their own gain. Some of you have small boards, some large boards. Think, too, about who is chairperson of your board—who runs the board meeting? Are the meetings peaceful or chaotic? Remember, these are people you listen to when trying to make a major decision, such as not doing drugs, going straight, getting along here at the prison. You don't have to fill all the chairs and you can add more if you need to. Any questions?

Leader: Let's talk about any reaction you had to drawing your board of directors?

Carl: I have a weird board—almost like there are two parts. I do have them on opposite sides of the table. I have a good family, and they want me to get straight with the Lord and live a good life. Then, I have two good friends who always get me to party with them, and that leads to trouble all the time. And I have a girlfriend who wants to get married, but she says I have got to quit the marijuana and get a real job.

Leader: Carl, who was chairperson of your board?

Carl: That's a good question. I don't know. Is it possible no one is? I feel like my board meetings are chaotic because no one is in charge.

Leader: Let's look at that in a few minutes. First, let's hear from some others.

Heidi: I am only seventeen but I feel like I am chairperson of my board, but I'm not strong enough to control the board members. I have all kinds of people telling me what to do. My grandparents are both on my board as are my parents. Also, I have one older sister and one older brother on my board. All these people want me to do well in school and become a lawyer because I am good at arguing. Then, I have three of my teammates and three real good friends I party with on my board, my boyfriend and even my ex-boyfriend. All want different things from me. No wonder I am a mess.

Emma: (*In a sad, confused voice*) I don't have anyone on my board except me. I don't listen to anyone tell me anything. I have always been this way—a lone wolf.

Frank: I hate to admit this, but my girlfriend is my chairperson. She's the reason I'm on house arrest. I listened to her, and I knew what we were doing was wrong. Most of my board members have quit. I need to get them back.

Leader: Every one of you seem to have gotten into this, and I think we will spend the rest of this session, and even the next one, talking about your board and changes you may want to make in it. Who wants to focus on something that you are thinking about as a result of doing your board of directors? (*Four hands go up.*) Who wants to go first?

Frank: I will.

The leader would go on and discuss the many different issues that arose from doing the board of director's exercise.

Getting It Behind You

This exercise works toward getting something finished or "behind you." Members are asked to write on a sheet of paper something that is always on their mind, such as early sexual abuse, guilt for what they did while using drugs, or a specific incident such as a shooting, divorce, or the harm they caused others. They are then asked to put the sheet about four-to-six inches from their face and stare at it. The leader can get all or some to comment on what they see other than what is on the page. (They see nothing but the page, which is the point of the exercise.)

The leader then directs the members to move the sheet to where at least one eye is seeing past the paper. After more discussion, the group members are instructed to put the sheet behind them and talk about what life would be like if they could get behind them what it is that is bothering them. (Caution—some may not want to say aloud what they have on the sheet.) Leaders using this exercise should expect much emotion and deep personal work. Thus, the leaders would need to be skilled at using counseling theories to help group members finish unfinished business. The exercise may stir up issues that members need to work on for the next few weeks. Also, this exercise can be done once or many different times during the life of a group since those in the correctional system often have more than one thing they need to get behind them.

Dyads and Triads

The use of dyads or triads (talking in pairs or threes) is another type of exercise that group leaders may use at various times and for a variety of reasons. Getting members to pair up often will cause them to focus since they are talking to just one other person. It also gives members a chance to talk about things to just one or two other persons—some find this easier than talking in front of the entire group.

Dyads can be used to warm members up to a topic, to finish with a topic, or for a change in the format. Dyads can be used when the leader wants to make sure all members get a chance to share their thoughts or feelings and there is not enough time to hear from everyone. Dyads also can be used when the leader needs time to think—that is, he can have members pair up and talk about something while he plans what to do next. Dyads also can be used when the leader wants to talk with a member. He can pair himself with that member and have members pair up with other members. Usually dyads last no more than five minutes. Leaders use triads when it seems like three people sharing will generate more discussion that just two people.

Example One: Dyad

Leader: We are going to spend most of the rest of the session talking about plans for when you get out. To start with, I am going to put you in pairs and have you share with each other the plans you have made since all of you will be out of here within a month. Tom and Bill pair up. Jon and Ed, and Matt and Corey. Spend about five minutes sharing your plans and then we'll talk in the large group.

Example Two: Dyad

Leader: A lot has been said about the incident. We need to move on to some other items, but I want us to close our discussion about the incident by letting you talk in pairs concerning what you are thinking about as a result of what has been said. We'll take about five minutes. Jane, pick someone to pair with.

Jane: Wanita.

Leader: Sue, you pick.

Sue: Edna.

Leader: Okay, that puts Donna and Jessica together. I want you to share thoughts, feelings, and reactions to the discussion.

Example Three: Triad

Leader: I could tell many of you were moved by the video. I am going to have you form groups of three and talk for about five minutes about what stood out. Everyone stand up. Now, get with two others. (*Leader watches to see that four groups of three form.*) Okay, you'll have about five minutes to share. . . . (*To end the triads, the leader gives a warning and then brings the members back to the large group.*) Take about thirty more seconds to finish. (*After thirty seconds*) Okay. Everyone finish up and come back to the large group. Who wants to share their discussion?

Movement Exercises

Movement exercises can be very useful in groups with members who are quiet or low on energy. Often, movement exercises get members "to speak with their bodies and motion" instead of with their mouths.

Movement exercises are also valuable because they are energizing; that is, the members get to move around instead of just sit. Movement exercises in this context are not dance, yoga, or going outdoors for some experiential-type exercise. In this case, movement allows members to get out of their seats and move around according to some instruction. We discuss five types of movement exercises: wall-to-wall continuums, moving to positions in a room, group sculpture, feedback lines, and drama scenes.

Wall-to-Wall Continuums

In the wall-to-wall continuum exercise, the leader instructs the members to line up behind one another in the middle of the room when one wall is designated as one thing and the other wall is designated as its opposite. The leader tells the members to move along the continuum to the position where they see themselves. Some examples of useful continuums include the following:

Leader———————————————Follower
Nurturing———————————————Critical
Winner———————————————Loser
Easy to know———————————————Hard to know
Working hard at recovery———————————————Not working at recovery
Working hard to better myself———————————————Just doing my time
Feel lots of guilt———————————————Feel no guilt
Feel lots of shame———————————————Feel no shame
Feel lots of anger———————————————Feel no anger
Feel lots of jealousy———————————————Feel no jealousy
Can depend on my family———————————————Can't depend on my family

There are many benefits from using this type of activity. It is energizing because the members are out of their seats. Also, members find it interesting to see where others put themselves. Additionally, when members take part by moving along any continuum, they are "speaking with their feet." This is a good exercise for drawing out members in that the leader can ask them about why they positioned themselves where they did. Leaders who have used this exercise have found that they can spend most of a session talking about reactions to doing one continuum. Some beginning leaders make the mistake of doing a number of continuums and not really processing any of them in depth.

Moving to Positions in a Room

Having members move to a spot in the room when they have a number of choices is another exercise that gets members up and moving. The leader identifies the positions in the room either verbally (pointing to different areas) or with written signs. One example of this comes from Transactional Analysis theory and the four "life" positions. The leader could have the members go to one of four spots that represent how they think of themselves and others.

I'm OK, You're not OK
I'm not OK, You're not OK
I'm not OK, You're OK
I'm OK, You're OK

Another example would be as follows:

I am going to mainly use AA and other support groups to keep me from drinking.
I am going to mainly use my family and friends to keep me from using.

I am going to mainly rely on myself to keep me from using.

I plan to use again but believe I will not get in trouble again.

Having members go to different parts of the room often helps stimulate discussion. Movement often seems to stimulate members to share more about what they believe or feel.

Group Sculpture

Another interesting movement exercise is what we call "group sculpture." In this exercise, one or some of the members are asked to position the other members according to how they see their participation in the group. The persons may be positioned with their back to the group, standing on a chair, holding tightly to two others, or whatever seems to indicate the way that person sees how others are involved. This can be a very powerful activity and can generate much discussion and many feelings. Leaders who employ this exercise should be prepared for some intense discussion and possible disagreements.

A variation of the group sculpture is to have members stand in a circle and then on the count of three, "sculpt" themselves as to how they see their participation. They might come to the center with arms open (representing being very open and into the group), stand where they are and put their hands over their ears, or turn their backs to the group and fold their arms. This can lead to a good discussion about how people feel about the group and how the group is going.

One well-known sculpture exercise is called "family sculpture." In this exercise, a member "sculpts" his family by placing other members who represent either the inmate's current family or the family when the inmate was growing up in positions that show how the family members relate to each other. This exercise, when done correctly, can evoke some deep-seated feelings and help members understand more about why they act the way they do. Members who are a part of the sculpture or who are just watching sometimes get as much or more than the member who is sculpting his family, which is why this exercise is considered so powerful.

Feedback Lines

The feedback line is another movement exercise where members give each other feedback by putting each other in a line. For example, the leader would ask one member to line up the other members according to how much the members are working to change. The member working the hardest to change would be put first and the one working the least would be put at the end. Also, lines can be formed around issues of trust—that is, putting the person they trust most at the front and the one they trust least at the end of the line. Other feedback lines could be placing members in order regarding those most likely to stay out of prison or most likely to stay sober. By giving feedback in this interesting way, members tend to pay lots of attention because they are being asked to move to different positions. This can be volatile; however, it can also be helpful for treatment groups that have enough trust and goodwill among the members to make it meaningful.

Drama Scenes

Drama scenes are another type of movement exercise that is quite effective. Acting out various scenes that are relevant to the group's purpose can prove to be very powerful and engaging for most if not all the members. Leaders sometimes have members act out visiting-room scenes, parenting scenes, or prison-living scenes. Members usually get involved with drama exercises because they are asked to play different parts in the drama. Members may be asked to play the supervisor, visiting family members, different people at a work site, or the parole board. The leader first gets the members to describe the scene, then the leader or members pick people for various parts. The leader would then help members who are going to play various people with their lines and actions. Having different members show how they would handle a situation usually leads to good discussion. Also, the members playing the parts can comment on how they felt. Drama exercises, when done well, usually are interesting and engaging for most if not all the members.

In addition to those mentioned, a number of other movement activities can be adapted to a correctional setting. Try various exercises and find the ones that work best for the population with whom you are working. You may want to almost always have a movement activity ready to use in case your group needs to be energized. Remember, using movement exercises helps to change the pace and energize the group.

Common Readings

A common reading consists of handing out a reading of one or two pages that everyone reads and then having members mark the one or two sentences that stand out. (The leader should know that all members are able to read, or the leader should make sure that the piece is read aloud by herself or another member.) The leader then generates discussion by asking members what they marked. By having the members mark something, it is much easier to call on them because most will feel comfortable sharing what they have underlined. The key with common readings is to get something that is interesting and filled with ideas that lead to discussion relevant to the purpose of the group. You may want to start collecting suitable readings now to have available when you lead groups. Such readings may come from church bulletins, through forwarded e-mails, from your own reading, and by asking friends and colleagues.

Experiential Exercises

Some exercises have an experiential component; that is, the members go and do something. Probably the best-known experiential activity is called the "ropes course." A ropes course is a collection of physically challenging exercises done outdoors that can only be completed if the group attempting them work together as a team. A ropes course is excellent for working with communication skills, conflict resolution, problem solving, and group support. Facilitators employ a method that involves:

- Having the group attempt the activity
- Stopping to discuss what is and is not working
- Then, attempting the activity again

By using these three steps, participants can see immediately how improvements in their behavior and skill can result in gains for themselves and the group. These activities can then be used to translate these skills into real-life situations and examples.

More challenging and intense activities exist. These include such activities as Outward Bound experiences, therapeutic wilderness experiences, high ropes courses, or climbing and canoeing courses. One advantage of such programs is that the offender does not have to be able to read or write to participate (Van Voorhis, Braswell, and Lester, 2000). These types of activities are excellent, especially for delinquent youth, because participants have to work cooperatively to accomplish tasks essential for survival. Martyn Whittingham, who has worked with delinquent youth for years, states: "There is tremendous value in having adolescents deal with situations that have immediate consequences like not working together on a high ropes course or not washing the pots and pans after a meal. Facilitators can then use these examples to discuss issues such as trust, choice, responsibility, seeking help, and acting on impulse. Also, skilled leaders can get the members to share what they are learning and how they can relate their behaviors to what can keep them out of jail or lead them to prison" (personal communication, 2002). More information about these types of activities can be found at *www.pa.org* or *www.aee.org*.

Values Clarification

One type of activity that helps group members become aware of what they believe is right and wrong and whether they operate on these beliefs is called "values clarification." These activities include discussion of questions that apply to various life situations and forced choice questions about certain issues. Listed on the next page are some possible values clarification exercises that could be introduced by using rounds, written responses, or wall-to-wall continuums.

- What would you do if you had six months to live?
- What would you do if you had five days to live?
- What would you take from your house if you knew your house was going to blow up in twenty minutes?
- Do you believe in life after death?
- Do you believe in extra-marital sex for you?
- Do you believe in extra-marital sex for your partner?
- What would you do if you found out your partner had an affair five years ago?
- What would you do if you found out your partner had an affair five days ago?
- What do you owe your parents?
- What brings you true happiness?
- Would you rather be thought of as a "tough" or a "good" person?
- It is never right to hit your partner/child—yes or no?

The list of values clarification exercises is endless. The benefit of these exercises is that they force the members to clarify what they believe and see how that may affect their behavior or see that their behavior is not congruent with what they say they believe. These exercises are most helpful with adolescents but are widely applicable.

Moral Dilemma Exercises

Moral dilemma exercises call for the members to decide something based on their belief system. In one example, the leader reads a piece about a lifeboat with a number of different people in it and two people need to be eliminated or the boat will sink. The members are asked whom they would eliminate. The different people may be a twenty-year-old addict, an eighty-year-old priest, a thirty-year-old addicted pregnant mom, a sixty-five-year-old senator, an eleven-year-old girl, a fifteen-year-old school dropout, a forty-five-year-old retired Hall of Fame baseball player, and so forth.

Another example of a moral dilemma exercise would be about finding $10,000 on a street corner. The members are asked what they would do. Another exercise concerns a good friend of yours who has AIDS and is planning to have unprotected sex with a person you do not know very well. Would you tell the person? These types of exercises often lead to a robust discussion about morals and values (Arbuthnot, 1984). These are especially good for certain adolescent groups (Gibbs, Arnold, Ahlborn, and Cheesman, 1984).

Group Decision Exercises

This type of exercise calls for the group to work together on a task or on answers to questions. An example of this involves the group being given a list of things that they could have if they were stranded in the winter after crash landing in a frozen place in Alaska. As a group they are to rank order the importance of the items. This type of activity can be useful for team building. Group decision exercises can be very useful for adolescents living in a halfway house or a wing of a detention center. The book *Joining Together* (Johnson and Johnson, 2000) has some excellent ideas for these types of activities.

Movies and Videotapes

A common activity in many prison educational groups and in some treatment groups is to show a movie or videotape. This activity is fine if the material in the videotape is relevant and current and if there is time spent discussing any thoughts or reactions to what was shown. Unfortunately, many leaders allow little or no time for discussion. Since the purpose of showing the film is to generate thoughts, feelings, questions, or reactions, skilled leaders make sure that there is time for processing, even if they have to show the movie in parts. Having members talk in dyads or triads or write down various reactions and then spend time in the whole group processing is a good way to maximize the value of showing a videotape or film.

Before showing a movie or videotape, it usually is best to spend two or three minutes telling the members what to look for and why they are seeing it. Important scenes may be obvious to you, but many of the members can easily miss the point of the film. Also, it is a good idea to think about processing questions ahead of time. Think of questions that can take them deeper into themselves. The leader who knows what questions to ask will not get sidetracked by irrelevant comments.

Trust Exercises

Trust is a major issue in correctional settings and has to be dealt with in most groups. The leader can help the group and individuals build trust. First, the leader should make sure that everyone talks, because if members are allowed to be silent, other members often become distrusting of that member. Two excellent ways to get members who are quiet to talk are to use rounds or movement exercises. Remember, quiet members in a prison group usually cause trust issues for the other members.

Another useful activity is to talk about trust because it helps members get a sense of how others feel about trust. Some of the issues leaders need to explore with their members are their feelings about trust when they were young and their history of being hurt by others. Another important topic is their feeling of trust for members in the group and for the leader. Listed next are some possible discussion questions or rounds that leaders can use to generate excellent discussions about trust.

- On a scale of 1-to-10, with 10 being very hard, how hard is it for you to trust the members of this group?
- On a scale of 1-to-10, with 10 being very hard, how hard is it for you to feel trust here in the prison?
- On a scale of 1-to-10, with 10 being very hard, how hard is it for you to trust people in your life?
- Whom have you trusted most in your life? Why?
- Whom do you trust in the group?
- Whom do you trust in the prison?
- What keeps you from trusting in the group?

For a group with members who are very distrusting, the leader can ask the members to rate their trust level in the group on a scale of 1-to-10 and have them write their number on a piece of paper to ensure anonymity. The leader would then read the ratings to the group. This should lead to a discussion, especially if some are high and some are low or if all are low. Leaders who are not sure of the members' trust for them may want to have the members rate their trust for them on a scale of 1-to-10 on a slip of paper.

If there is lack of trust between certain members, leaders may want to pair members who do not trust each other and have them talk about trust or the issue being discussed. This sometimes can help to diffuse a negative trust situation between them, but leaders have to be very careful because this can backfire and the members can become very hostile. Definitely a leader would want to monitor their interaction by paying particular attention to their conversation as they listen to the various dyads. The leader may even want to spend time in the dyad working with them on their lack of trust for each other.

Most of the time, these exercises help to increase trust in a group. One of the best ways to develop trust in a group is to have the group be helpful. Getting members to say helpful and encouraging things to other members and cutting off negative comments help to develop trust. However, at times, nothing will work and the leader, if possible, should screen out a member to increase trust so that the group can be valuable for the other members. If you ever find yourself in a situation where you cannot screen out members who create a distrusting atmosphere, then you will have to work extra hard to have the experience be meaningful for most members. Too often, correctional workers give up and just go through the motions of meeting as a group, with everyone, including the leader, hating the experience. This does not have to happen. Creative, skilled leaders can have a productive group when trust is rather low.

Using Purchased Programs

Many correctional institutions purchase "canned" programs that include numerous exercises. The institution mandates that leaders use the activities in these programs. Because there are so many of these used by the Federal Bureau of Prisons and different state prison systems, we will not describe them here. Some readers are probably using some purchased programs mandated by the institution. Often, the ideas and information are very helpful and can be used as the manual says. At other times, the material will need to be modified for the specific group being led because it is not completely relevant for the members. Skilled leaders will modify the material so that it fits the group, whereas the unskilled leaders obediently do everything the manual indicates, even if they sense it will not be helpful. Pollock (1998) states: "Not all programs work for all prisoners. Counselors should stay out of a 'box' of rote program assignments for offenders. Sometimes a prison will run a particular program for years with no attempt to evaluate it" (p.141).

Concluding Comments

A skilled leader uses many different types of exercises when leading groups in correctional settings. In this chapter, we discussed rounds, written exercises, dyads and triads, movement exercises, common readings, experiential exercises, values clarification, moral dilemma exercises, group decision exercises, movies and videotapes, trust exercises, and purchased programs. Through readings, workshops, and course work, you will be exposed to many different exercises. We encourage you to start developing a list of exercises that you like and that you think would work in different correctional situations.

Using Props in Creative Exercises

In the last chapter, we discussed different types of exercises. In this chapter, we discuss additional exercises, using props. Props include such things as a shield, a filter, a large beer bottle, a cassette tape, or a Styrofoam cup. The props are used as a way to get members focused. For instance, a leader can hold up a piece of Plexiglas as a shield and ask members, "When do you need a shield in your interactions with people?" Members immediately start to think of the hostile or negative people in their lives from whom they need to block comments. Exercises using various props are quick, valuable, and memorable because members tend to remember things they look at or hold in their hands.

In two previous books, Jacobs (1992; 1994) discussed the benefits of using a multisensory approach in counseling. Props can be used as a way to get members to understand, visualize, or get in touch with something they are doing or can do. Once you are comfortable with the idea of using props, you probably will be able to think of many that can be helpful in your groups. The key to successful use of props is in understanding the theory that is illustrated by them. In this chapter, we provide examples of the use of props.

Shield

In correctional settings, people need to deflect negative or hostile comments that are aimed at them by some inmates, officers, and family members. The shield exercise consists of the leader introducing the concept of how people may need to use a shield in their lives to block out comments from people. For the exercise, the shield can be a clipboard, a book, a piece of Plexiglas, or any other sturdy object that can deflect things. We like using the Plexiglas because a member can see through it.

Example: Shield

It is about thirty minutes into a session for members who live at a halfway house. The topic of how other people hurt them has been discussed for the last few minutes. The leader decides to use the shield to make his point.

Leader: Since many of you have talked about hostile or negative people in your life, including some here at the halfway house, I thought of an exercise we could do. See this piece of Plexiglas? I want you each to think of it as a shield and think of when you need a shield in your life. For me, I know when I am around my grandparents I always need a shield, because they are very critical of me and everyone else. Let me show you this. Joe, stand up here with me. I want you to think of Joe as my grandfather and his pokes as negative comments. I want you to poke at me, and I am going to deflect the pokes with the shield.

Joe, when you are poking, I want you to say some of the things my grandfather used to say to me, like "You'll never amount to anything. You're lazy. You're no good. Quit acting like a girl." (*Joe does this and everyone watches.*) Joe's not hurting me because I am using my shield. Now, back to all of you. When do you need a shield against negative people in your lives, and when will you need one when you are on your own again?

Clem: I needed one when I was growing up. I hated being around my dad when he was drunk. My dad said all those things your grandfather said to you and more.

Leader: Let me comment on that, because I think it applies to a number of you in here. People who grow up around alcoholics often need a shield. *(Picks up a large, three-foot, heavy plastic beer bottle*) Clem, come up here. You take the shield and hold it tight. I want you to block my attacks when I try to poke you with this bottle. (*Pokes at Clem with the bottle. Clem deflects the bottle which makes a rather loud noise as it hits the shield.*) "Clem, you're no good. You are stupid. You are lazy and never are going to amount to anything. What a waste you are."

Clem: (*Excitedly*) That's exactly what happened in my home, but I didn't have the shield.

Leader: Who wants to tell us about how they need a shield now? We'll try to cover everyone today, and if we don't get to everyone, we'll finish up at our next meeting. Knowing when to use a shield is so very important.

(Members share for the next few minutes about how they needed and still need a shield in their lives. Sam asks an important question that gives the leader a chance to explain that the shield is actually changing self-talk.)

Sam: This is interesting, but I can't take a shield home with me. What am I going to do, hold up a clipboard when my dad goes off on me?

Leader: There are some things you could do, like pick up a book to remind you to shield the comments but the real shielding comes in what you are telling yourself. Remember how we talked about the idea that it is our thoughts that cause our feelings.

Members: Yeah (*some nod*).

Leader: Your shield is truthful self-talk. If you say to yourself, "There goes grandpa being his negative self. He does not really know me."

Ted: What if it is true?

Leader: Well, that is something different. For our discussion here, try to think of people who say things that need to be deflected because they are negative, hostile, exaggerated, or just unkind.

Ronnie: Every time I get a visit from my mom, she starts in on me. I want her to visit because she is going to die soon, but I hate it when she attacks me.

Leader: Let's look at how you can shield those comments and tell yourself something different. What does your mom say?

Ronnie: She always says I'm no good. I'm nothing and always will be nothing!

Leader: Let's look at the truth. (*To the group*) What can Ronnie put on his shield? What does he need to tell himself?

Clem: That he made mistakes and paid for them, and he can be something. Just like that dude that came and talked to us. Look at him. He's got his own company now, and he really did some bad stuff early in his life.

Leader: Ronnie, do you believe Clem?

Ronnie: Yeah, I do feel like doing time was the best thing for me. I sure was heading nowhere. With all these skills I have picked up, I know I can get a good job.

Leader: I want to write on this Post-it note something that needs to go on your shield. (*Writes I can be somebody! I am somebody who is going to make it! Hands note to Ronnie.*)

Ronnie: What do I do with this?

Leader: Stick it on the shield so you can read it. (*Ronnie does this.*) All of us need a shield at one time or another. I want all of you to understand that your self-talk really is the shield. (*Everyone is paying attention; many seem deep in thought.*)

Not only is the shield useful for members when they interact with family members, but it is also a very good image to use if there are many hostile interactions at the correctional institution where they live. By teaching the use of a shield, some members may avoid situations that eventually lead to a fight or an unpleasant confrontation.

Filter

The use of a filter is similar to the use of a shield, but it is a better metaphor when having to deal with persons who are negative but who also must be listened to because they are the supervisor, parent, warden, and so forth. A filter can be used to teach about letting certain things through and filtering out the rest when dealing with staff, family, or other inmates.

Example: Filter

This is a group in a prison and the members are complaining about how unfair certain staff members are. The leader wants to show that the inmates are going to have to learn to live with this so she decides to use a filter to make her point.

Leader: I agree that some of the staff are not always fair and certainly not always nice, but you can learn to live with it. I know this because I have seen prisoners come here and fight, argue, and complain, and I have seen some figure out that that is how so and so is and they filter most of what he or she is saying. (*Holds up a furnace filter.*) You have a choice to filter a lot of what is being said and stay reasonably calm, or you can react to everything and find yourself in lots of trouble. (*Puts down the filter. Members stare at it.*)

Pam: (*Angrily*) They have no right to treat me the way they do!

Leader: (*Holds up the filter again*) Pam, I wish some of the people who work here would be kinder, but that's who they are and they are not going to get fired. You can filter what they say. How do you think Ginger is able to work with the people she works with and not get bent out of shape?

Pam: I don't know. Ginger, how do you do it?

Ginger: By using a mental filter. I just listen to the job assignments and I don't pay attention to the rest. My counselor taught me the filter thing after I nearly punched one of the cooks. Now, I filter their crap.

Leader: Do others of you see where a filter would be helpful?

Jude: I do. I need one when Smitty is in charge. Smitty says the stupidest ass things! He gets me so mad.

Leader: That's where a filter is needed.

Della: What are you really talking about? We can't carry a filter.

Leader: But you can carry the image in your mind to remind you to use your filter, even prepare ahead of time to be ready to use your filter when you know you are going to be interacting with someone whose words needs to be filtered. (*Some laugh*) Ginger, explain to them when and how you use your filter.

In this example, discussion would take place regarding how to use the filter. Each person could be asked to talk about situations where she needed a filter. Ideally, the leader would have taught the members theories such as REBT and TA because they would be very useful in the discussion of how to use the filter. Looking at the self-talk and the different ego states involved would be quite helpful in gaining an understanding of ways to filter interactions that are negative or hostile.

Exploding Pop Bottle

Anger is definitely an issue that is addressed in many treatment groups in correctional settings. One way to focus members on their anger is for the leader to get a full, plastic pop bottle and shake it while talking to the members. They will wonder what the leader is doing. Then, the leader would give it to a member and ask that member to open it. This leads to discussion of how a person can release the pressure slowly or can "spew" all over everyone.

Example: Exploding Pop Bottle

During a weekly probation group, the leader wants to focus on controlling anger since many of the members have brought up this subject. It is about twenty minutes into the session.

Leader: (*Shaking a full pop bottle*) Many of you feel that your anger is uncontrollable, or that it just builds up and you have to let it go and it spews everywhere. Often, your anger is not really directed at the person who gets it. Frequently, you are angry about something that happened earlier in the day with a letter or the parole board. (*Still shaking the bottle*) So, if I asked you to open this bottle, would you do it?

Bob: No way!

Joe: I'll open it and aim at Fred. (*People laugh.*)

Leader: Can you just get it on Fred?

Fred: You aren't spraying that on me!

Vinny: Are you really going to have us open it?

Leader: If anyone opens it, you can only aim it at yourself. Anyone who wants to open it can. You get to drink it.

Bob: I'm not opening it.

David: Can I open it now? I want to. Can I open it slowly to let the fizz out?

Leader: If you want to try it that way.

David: (*Takes the bottle and slowly opens and closes the cap until the pressure has been released. All watch and some sitting nearby move away.*) If I take my time, I'm going to have a free pop.

Leader: David is right on. How does this relate to anger management?

Vinny: We need to learn to release our pressure in ways that don't make a mess. Great image for me!

The leader would then ask various members to comment. She would try to deepen the discussion to explore what the members can do to release pressure rather than "spewing" their anger all over everyone. Some examples would be taking a time out, counting to 10 or even to 100, practicing some type of relaxation breathing, writing in a journal, or challenging their negative self-talk.

Fuses

In Chapter 2 we presented a brief example where the leader used different pieces of string or cord to represent various lengths of "anger fuses." This is a good exercise when dealing with anger because members quickly relate to the idea of having a short fuse or the need to lengthen their fuse. Many leaders of anger management groups use the fuse in the first session as a way to frame the purpose of the group, which is to lengthen every member's fuse. By having available some very short fuses and some medium fuses and some long fuses, the leader can make reference to the need for people to have longer fuses.

Example: Fuses

This is a group of teenage girls who are in a detention center. It is the first session of a group on anger, about fifteen minutes into the session.

Leader: (*Throws out twenty or so pieces of thick string of lengths varying from one inch to one foot.*) I want you to think about how long your anger fuse is. Pick the string which represents the length of your anger fuse.

Helen: Mine's the shortest one out there.

Leader: Fine, pick one.

Diane: Mine is short too.

Dedra: Mine is a little longer than it used to be but still is short.

Sandra: I don't think it is good to have that long one.

Leader: We are going to talk about all this in the group. That's why it is called an anger management group. I assume you signed up for this group because you wanted a longer fuse. Am I right?

Sandra: I need better control of my anger, but I don't want you to turn me into some wimp.

Leader: I can promise that won't happen, but we will be talking about lengthening your fuse.

Traci: I have a short fuse! I don't think I can change much—not to that long one.

Leader: I just want you to look at the long fuse and tell me what you imagine that would be like.

The leader centers much of the discussion around the length of the fuses and the problems associated with having a short one. Also, discussion would eventually be about how to lengthen the fuse. One theory we recommend on dealing with anger is REBT.

Cassette Tapes

Cassette tapes can be used as a way of letting people know that they can change. The leader can hold up an old and a new cassette tape or can give each member an old tape and one that is still wrapped.

Example: Cassette Tapes

This group is for inmates at a minimum-security prison. The leader wants to focus on getting the members to see that they can change if they change their thinking.

Leader: I want you each to look at these two cassette tapes. What is different about them?

Julie: One is new and one is old.

Leader: Right. Now, what do you think is on the new one?

Paula: Nothing. It's never been opened.

Leader: So, we can put whatever we want to on the new one? (*Members nod.*) Let's talk about the old one. If the old tape had some bad stuff on it and you took it out of the player and put in the good one, would you hear the bad stuff?

Cindy: If it is out, then you won't hear it. You might hear it some in your head.

Leader: That's true. But if you played a new tape over and over again, don't you think the old one would fade?

Ruby: What's your point? You always use things to make a point.

Leader: My point is that many of you have old tapes in your head about you not being worthwhile and not deserving to be happy. You play the tape all the time. (*Holds up the old tape; members stare at it.*) What this group can be about and what your time in prison can be about is making a new tape.

Julie: I can't just forget all the crap that has happened to me.

Leader: That's not what I am saying. I am saying most of you play all kinds of negative tapes in your head about yourself. You all can make a new tape starting right now, based on who you are now and what you are doing. (*The leader is now holding the new tape in one hand and the old tape in the other.*) The old tape is based on what was done to you and what you did.

The leader would center discussion around the idea of making a new tape and would get members to discuss their beliefs about the possibility of making a new tape. The leader would also discuss how their old tape was made and how they can make a new one based on current information. The use of the tapes to drive home the point that they can change by making new tapes can be quite powerful to some members. The leader may mention that the purpose of the group sessions is to help them make new tapes that will keep them out of prison once they are released. This is a way of teaching the concept that negative thinking is learned, not innate, which is supported by many theories, including TA, REBT, and Adlerian theory.

Large Beer Bottle

An excellent prop for working with alcohol problems is a large plastic beer bottle (about three feet tall, sold in novelty stores as a coin bank). The large beer bottle can be put in the center of the group with a small beer bottle and members can look at the two and give their thoughts about how big their problem is. The leader can ask each member to comment. Another activity that can get members' attention is to take money and small dolls representing kids and family and drop them into the large bottle. The members get to see how everything goes into the bottle when they are alcoholic.

A strong visual image for members to see how alcohol inhibits closeness is to get two members to stand in the center of the group and have one member be a person who drinks and the other be a spouse, friend, parent, or sibling. Have the two members place the three-foot bottle between them while they try to hug. This shows how the bottle keeps people from getting close. Another visual activity is to have one person hold the large bottle with both hands and then ask him or her to hug another member who represents a significant person in the drinking member's life. The person cannot hug the other without letting go of the large bottle. All these demonstrations can generate much discussion and often pain about how alcohol is affecting relationships with others.

Dollar Bill

A goal of many treatment groups is to help members feel more worthwhile since many inmates feel less worthwhile as a result of being in prison or as a result of all the negative things that they have done or that have happened to them. One way to make the point that they are worthwhile and nothing can make them less worthwhile is to use a dollar bill.

Example: Dollar Bill

The leader wants to focus on self-worth and how nothing can cause the inmates to be less worthwhile. It is thirty minutes into the session.

Leader: From what you have been saying, it sounds to me like many of you think you are less worthwhile than others who are on the outside or even some who are here at the detention center. Raise your hands if you think that. (*Nearly all hands go up.*)
Carter: My dad always said I was no good! Not worth anything and never would amount to anything!
Leader: Carter, come up here. (*They both stand in front of the group.*) I want all of you to think about this for yourself as I do this demonstration with Carter. (*Leader takes out a dollar bill and holds it up.*) Carter, how much is this worth?
Carter: A dollar.
Leader: (*Crumples the dollar bill; hits it, steps on it, hits it some more, then unfolds it.*) How much is this now worth, even though it has been beaten and kicked around? I could even go lock it up for a while.
Carter: (*Takes a few seconds to think*) Still a dollar.

Leader: Exactly! Nothing can take your worth away! Do you see my point?

Rex: I don't get it. You just put the dollar through hell.

Joey: I think I do. You're saying that we are not worth less than others, no matter what hell we've been through.

Leader: What do others of you think about what Joey's saying and about my demonstration?

The dollar bill image is one that often sticks with inmates and helps to drive home the point that they are equal to everyone else even though they are in prison and have been told all kinds of things while growing up. Another value of this exercise is that the leader can refer back to it at other times, reminding members that they are worthwhile. Incidentally, when working with inmates, the issue of being worthwhile underlies many of their problems. Leaders must clearly understand this and be able to address the issue directly with group members. The use of the dollar bill illustrates the humanistic perspective that all humans are worthwhile and that no matter what, the person's worth does not change.

Rearview Mirror

One of the goals of treatment groups is to get members to look toward a positive future. A rearview mirror can be used as an exercise that leads to discussion about the future. For this exercise, the leader has the members take the rearview mirror and hold it up in front of them, either directly in front so that it is the only thing they see or off to the side where they see in front of them and also can glance in the mirror. After they do this, the leader would have the members talk about how they are living now—is the mirror totally in front of them so all they see is their past, or is the mirror off to the side? This can lead to insightful discussion about the past and future and how to see the past. The rearview mirror demonstrates the perspective that the past does not have to be the determining factor in their future; that they can, with conscious effort and determination, live in the present and improve their future.

Poker

Many in correctional settings feel like they have to "play the hand they were dealt." Inmates often feel they have come from a poor socioeconomic or family situation that was so bad that nothing can change the course of their lives. They have a sense of helplessness about taking steps to free themselves from their past or present influences. They feel that nothing can help them, and certainly not anyone within the "system."

An exercise that is good for discussing this concept uses the card game of poker. (Even if you don't know how to play poker, you can just focus on two-of-a-kind, three-of-a-kind or four-of-a-kind.) To ensure you get them to focus on their "bad hand," fix the deck so that the hand you deal each person or one or two members is a bad hand—no pairs. (Depending on the size of the group, you may just want to have a couple of members and you play while the others watch.)

With the hand you deal yourself, you take cards until you get a decent hand. No one else gets to take cards, because they have to play the hand they were dealt. You can continue to play more hands for yourself, but they have to keep their "bad hand," and you continue to take cards. They most likely will say it's not fair and you can comment about how they have said "This is who I am" or "This is the hand I was dealt." You can ask them how to get a better hand. Usually, someone will say "Get new cards." You can have them ask for specific cards which you can go through the deck and find. This leads to discussion about how they can change their hand and how they do not have to play the hand they were dealt. Also, you can discuss how you helped them improve their hand and how you can help them improve their lives if they seek help and ask for it directly.

Small Child's Chair

As we discussed in Chapter 6, one of the most valuable props for helping people see another part of themselves is a small child's chair that can be sat in by adolescents and adults. This concept comes from the TA theory and also is illustrative of the REBT idea of the irrational part of us that replays untrue and upsetting self-talk. The small chair can be used in exercises in many ways.

Using the chair to represent the little boy or little girl gives members a concrete image of the part of themselves that feels angry, guilty, hurt, worthless, or scared. The small chair can be placed in the center of the group, and the question can be asked, "When do you find yourself acting out of this chair while here at this place?" Or, members can be asked "Growing up, when did you find yourself in the small chair, and how did you act?" The leader can have members look at the chair or actually sit in it. Many times, people tell us how sitting in the chair really had an impact on them—getting them to go deeper into themselves because they feel small. The chair can be used to get members to think about when they are in the small chair with family or friends or at a work site. (One caution: The chair should never be used to embarrass or humiliate a member.) The important thing is that the chair usually will generate much discussion and also serve as a focus point; that is, people will continue to stare at it and stay focused on the Child part of themselves. We know people remember it because we often hear members say, "I stayed out of the little chair this week" or "I almost went to the small chair, but I stopped myself!"

Example: Small Child's Chair

The group has been discussing their different feelings and how they do not understand why they act the way they do. The leader decides to focus them further on their feelings.

Leader: I want us to do this exercise. First, look at the small chair I'm putting here in the center. The chair represents the part of you that feels angry, hurt, not okay. I want you to think about when you find yourself in that chair. Knowing you like I do, I know that many of you live in that seat more than this seat (*puts a regular-size chair next to the small chair in the center of the group with a big THINK sign on it*). Just look at the little chair and share any thoughts and feelings.

Billy Joe: I think I must be in it all the time. Everyone says I walk around here angry at the world.

Leader: You are in it a lot. Even in this group, you often are in the small chair wanting to argue or put someone else down. Billy Joe, you are in the thinking seat right now, because you really are thinking. I hope you can see that you have a choice as to which seat to sit in.

Felix: I am in that little seat at my job site and when I am in the classroom. I feel no good, that others are smarter and faster than I am.

Saddam: I am like that too, especially with school, since my English is not so good.

Harry: I don't like it that you are telling us that we act like little kids. We're all at least sixteen. We're not kids!

David: Harry, he's not calling us anything. He is trying to help us see how we act. I am in the little seat when my folks come to visit. I have always been in this seat when I am around them. They love Jerry and Judy more than me. (*Gets up and goes and sits in it; most laugh*) Gee, this feels weird. I feel small, like a kid.

Leader: David, we can work on getting you out of that seat. Others of you may want to sit in it. You may get in touch with some more feelings. I am going to leave it there the rest of this session. Other thoughts and feelings?

By using the chairs as part of an exercise, the leader has generated feelings and thoughts that can be discussed for the entire session. By doing this, most of the members will remember the concept of being in the small chair. The leader will use the chair in later sessions as well, either as an exercise or when working with one member on an issue when he is acting out his Child part. The proper use of the small chair can generate tremendous insight, motivation, and energy.

Concluding Comments

In this chapter, we present a few ways that props can be used in exercises. However, it is important to understand that there are an unlimited number of props that you can use in groups that will cause members to think and go deeper into themselves. We believe props should be used frequently because people tend to remember more when they see or feel something. Using props will add to the effectiveness and impact of your groups. In our classes, we have our students use props in practice sessions just to get them comfortable with the idea. Some are hesitant at first, but almost all are comfortable by the end of the semester and comment how valuable props are in the groups they are leading outside of class.

Special Populations and Personality Types in Correctional Settings

One of the fascinating aspects of working in a correctional setting is the variety of personality types and populations leaders encounter. While correctional staff must always be aware of the challenges each presents, the competent group leader understands and prepares for the particular needs of, and influences of, special populations when leading groups. In this chapter, we address some personality characteristics that are common to the general population found in correctional work, and we also discuss some specific subgroups. Some correctional settings may have concentrations of one or two of these specific populations.

Personality Types

The Con/Liar

Some members of correctional groups will lie and try to con the group leader and other group members. This makes leading difficult because the leader is never sure if what the person is saying is the truth or a con. With all inmates, leaders will want to be alert to being conned. For some inmates, lying and conning are ways of life, and leaders always have to remind themselves that a particular member may be conning them. Often, other members challenge a member who is lying or conning and with experience, group leaders will get better at detecting this. However, at times no member picks up on or cares to challenge the lying, and some may even encourage and support it. Much conning can and most likely will occur if the leader is not paying careful attention to this possibility (Silverman and Vega, 1996).

The Angry or Volatile Member

In a correctional population, members in groups may impulsively attack, verbally or physically, anyone in the group with the slightest provocation. Prior to leading the group, all group leaders need to think, will this topic be volatile? They need to think about who might blow up over something being said in the session. We are not saying to avoid the topics, but we are saying, **Be Prepared**. Many times, if leaders make the group interesting enough, volatile members become more cooperative and less combative. The key is not to force the angry/volatile member early on; give the member time to ease into the group. Early confrontation usually results in a bad outcome (Walsh, 2001).

No matter how much leaders prepare, at times things will escalate in groups. The challenge is for leaders to maintain a calm and logical demeanor while trying to settle down and defuse a potentially violent situation. Stepping out of that calm realm and becoming defensive or angry can escalate the situation to the point where it becomes violent.

Leaders have many choices when they are confronted with a member who is starting to attack others in the group. However, it is essential that they use a calm voice. Most importantly, they should not let the situation get out of hand. If leaders find themselves in a potentially bad situation, there are a number of things they can do:

- They can put members in dyads and pair themselves with the angry member.
- They can put members in dyads and pair up the two who are having trouble and join their dyad.
- They can stop the group immediately and then talk with the members involved.
- They can ask the member(s) to leave.
- They can get the other members to focus on what is happening by asking them what they see, then seek input from members who are likely to defuse the volatile situation.
- They can hit their panic button to get immediate help.

Once out of the situation, the leader will need to decide what to do about the volatile member. If the leader believes that the member is not ready to benefit from the group and that he is harming the group process, it is the leader's responsibility to eliminate the member from the group. The experienced group leader is willing to screen out a member. Leaders always want to make sure that they do not sacrifice the group out of fear of hurting one member's feelings.

The Very Quiet Member

A common personality type in correctional settings is the very quiet individual. When such a person is placed in a group, that individual's presence can have a negative effect on the rest of group because other members are uncomfortable with the person's silence. When a leader is faced with having the quiet person in his or her group, it is important to determine why the member is quiet and then to figure out if the person wants to participate more or if the group can adjust to having the quiet person in the group. Meeting privately with the inmate is usually the best way to find out why the person is so quiet. Once the leader has this meeting, the member may feel more comfortable about speaking up. The leader may be able to share in group (with the quiet member's permission) why the member is so quiet, or the leader may ask the member to not be in the group. The leader is responsible for creating the best learning environment possible, and it is the leader's obligation to determine if the person should be allowed to stay in the group (Walsh, 2001).

Although completely quiet members can benefit from being present in a group, even if they do not volunteer much personal information, they usually will benefit much more if they share. More importantly, a totally quiet member can keep others from sharing at any meaningful level.

In a correctional setting, members may be quiet for many reasons:

- They have a serious problem with trust.
- They are not liked.
- They believe that they are not liked by others.
- They fear they will be ridiculed.
- They may be mentally challenged and find it difficult to keep up with the pace of a discussion.

- They may be under some threat if they speak, either from another member or from someone outside the group.
- They completely resent being in the group and have no interest in participating.

By understanding why members are quiet, the leader may be able to help them to decide to be more active participants.

The Totally Uncooperative Member

Leaders will meet uncooperative members during their work in corrections. Some leaders make the mistake of spending a lot of time trying to get them to talk by asking them questions or focusing attention on them or letting them talk about completely irrelevant topics. Each of these strategies is worth trying, but skilled leaders can quickly assess whether their drawing-out attempts are working. If they are not working, the leader moves on to other members and lets the uncooperative member sit more or less quietly. Sometimes, the other members understand that the one member does not want to participate, so his silence is accepted and does not greatly harm the trust or comfort level in the group. If, on the other hand, the uncooperative member's presence is disruptive, then the member should be screened out of the group if possible (Walsh, 2001).

The Mentally Challenged Member

Jails and prisons are filled with a number of mentally challenged individuals. By "mentally challenged," we mean those having very low IQs or suffering from brain damage or some form of mental illness. Ideally, these members would be in groups together, but this often is not the case. In most instances, the mentally challenged inmates are put in a group with inmates who do not have these limitations. This can cause problems for leaders. Some leaders make the mistake of catering to the pace of the mentally challenged members, which ends up boring most of the other members of the group. Other leaders ignore these members, which causes them to either act out or feel discounted and rejected.

Walsh (2001) devotes an entire chapter to dealing with the mentally ill and mentally deficient offenders. He describes how the correctional worker must be prepared to deal effectively with offenders who are especially ill-equipped to respond positively to counseling. The best solution is to deal with these inmates in their own group if at all possible. Careful screening should allow the leader to be able to determine if an inmate is low functioning and then, if possible, these offenders can be placed in a group that is appropriate for them. If this is not possible, cater more to those who are not mentally challenged, but try to be sensitive to the needs of the mentally challenged members and whenever possible, use the other members to work with, help, and explain things to the challenged inmates.

Other Populations

In this section, we briefly discuss specific populations based on gender, age, and cultural background. This information is an overview, and thorough coverage of each of these topics can be found in other books and on various web sites. Our purpose here is to introduce these populations and urge leaders to do more specific work in the areas that are appropriate to them.

Women

Many correctional workers are asked to lead groups that consist only of women. To lead these groups effectively, leaders need to understand the women they have in their groups. Pollock (1998) and Wojda and Rowse (1997) have written excellent books on women in prisons. According to Pollock, most of the women in prison are uneducated, come from a background involving physical and sexual abuse, are slightly older, have at least one child, have minimal criminal histories, and are responsible for less than 10 percent of violent crime. They are generally unemployed at the time of arrest and tend to have worked in low-paying, gender in traditional jobs and have low self-esteem. For those who are interested learning more of the demographics of women in prison, Pollock (1998) and Snell (1994) both provide in-depth discussions.

One major problem for women who are involved with the penal system is that most are mothers. According to Wojda and Rowse (1997), the most common concerns voiced by mothers in prison revolve around what is happening to their children while they are gone. Correctional workers need to realize that this topic will come up in many of the groups that are led in correctional settings and group leaders need to be aware of all the different issues and concerns of these mothers (Morton and Williams, 1998; Blinn, 1997). Prison counselors often conduct groups with mothers, focusing solely on separation issues (Clement, 1993).

Another helpful group to conduct for woman is a group for mothers who give birth to their babies while in prison but are separated from them immediately (Kauffman, 2001). The leader of such groups needs to be very sensitive to the issues of separation from children. For those mothers who have their babies taken away almost immediately, group leaders need to be prepared to deal with depression, guilt, and anger. Ideally, both psychoeducational groups about parenting from prison and counseling groups should be conducted for these women.

A few programs are allowing incarcerated women opportunities to bond with their newborn infants by allowing them to reside in special centers for several months to a year (Blinn, 1997). Leaders of these groups must know about infant care and child development so they can provide effective leadership.

Other groups that are helpful specifically to women are those that deal with sexual trauma, codependency, and self-esteem. Special knowledge and skill are required for each of these concerns, especially sexual trauma. Correctional workers should get training in dealing with sexual trauma if they plan to lead groups with women because this subject will come up often in treatment groups.

Self-esteem groups are important because many women in prison feel bad about themselves and believe that women should follow a man's direction. It is important that education and treatment groups for women foster autonomy from men and raise the women's self-esteem. A goal of group counseling with women in corrections is to encourage them to set and achieve personal goals that will help them feel confident that they can make it on their own so that they will not follow a man into crime again.

Most women find sharing in groups to be well within their comfort range (Pollock, 1998). Women are more likely than men to engage in talking openly in a group because verbalizing problems is a typical form of problem solving among women. However, some will not talk. Often, these are women who have become involved in what has been termed "pseudo-families," forming a subculture almost like a family or a gang (Heffernan, 1972; Silverman and Vega, 1996; Ward and Kassebaum, 1965). The subculture meets their needs, so these women are more distrustful of staff, less introspective, and not as apt to see that their lives need improvement (Owen, 1998). Understanding this subculture and the attitudes that it breeds can help a leader plan for these women's resistance due to their not feeling the need for a group to fulfill their sense of affiliation or belonging (Ward and Kassebaum, 1965).

Men working with women in groups need to be aware of many possible problems. Since many of the women were either sexually abused by men, battered by men, or led into crime by men, they will have trust issues that will need to be addressed. The best thing for the male correctional worker to do is to be very sensitive to this and make sure that he is kind, caring, and understanding. The male leader also has to be prepared for the women to "come on" to him, and he has to always be ethical and appropriate (Pollock, 1998).

Men

Generally speaking, the "traditional" male is not likely to seek groups with whom to share feelings or concerns. In fact, most men have a strong resistance to what most inmates believe happens in groups. Sharing in groups is sometimes ridiculed. Kassebaum, Ward, and Wilner (1971) found that men were afraid to reveal too much about themselves because they were concerned that both staff and inmates would use it against them. Many inmates felt it was "unmanly" to talk about feelings and discomforts. The experienced leader understands that one of their tasks is to sell traditional men on the value and benefits of being in a group. One way to get men interested in being in a treatment group where personal sharing occurs is to first have them participate in classes or psycho-educational groups where the sharing is not as personal.

Women who lead all-male groups in correctional settings may need to prove their ability to be strong and clear before male members will trust them. Men who lead male groups need to be strong, yet not so strong that they cause the members to clam up or rebel. Later in this chapter, we discuss sex offenders and batterers groups, which are frequently all-male groups.

Cocorrectional Groups

In some settings, such as halfway houses or other treatment centers, there will be a mix of men and women. This can be a valuable experience if the leader can get the members to focus on themselves and the different topics. Often, in mixed groups, the men and women may not focus on the purpose of the group, especially when they are seeking the approval or attention of the opposite gender. Managing the sexual energy at times can be challenging, especially with adolescents; members sometimes are so bold as to even try to fondle each other under the table. The best way to eliminate this temptation is to remove the table. The leader who stays focused on the different topics and makes the material interesting and relevant usually can manage these groups effectively.

If at all possible, leaders of mixed groups should make participation optional. Careful screening should be done to make sure that members are comfortable sharing with members of the opposite sex.

Adolescents

Dealing with juvenile offenders or youthful offenders (those juveniles sentenced as adults) is another specialty. We address briefly some of the important issues here but strongly recommend that those who are interested in this population seek out workshops and reading on dealing with juveniles or youthful offenders specifically (*see* Jackson, 1998; Glick and Sturgeon, 2002). One important point to understand when dealing with adolescents is that peer pressure is a major influence in their lives. This is where the group can prove to be extremely valuable if the leader has the skill to get the members interested and engaged in meaningful discussion. While teenagers are suited for group interaction and learning due to their developmental stage, their general high level of energy and lack of focus require endless patience. The trick is to harness their interests by generating stimulating discussion on topics that are relevant to the adolescent population. It is important to have a solid plan, a clear sense of purpose, strong cut-off skills, and knowledge about the area of focus.

Adolescents in correctional settings struggle with their conflicting feelings toward authority figures and their peers. These conflicting feelings occur often during group interactions. Frequently, adolescents send a mixed message—"I like you and I hate you"—to everyone in the group, especially the leader. Leaders should not take this personally. Also, it is important that leaders not abdicate their leadership in hopes of being liked. Leaders of adolescent groups may need to exercise their authority to keep the group focused. Remember, these adolescents resist authority and yet they need a strong authority figure.

Trust exercises work well with adolescents since trust is such a big issue for them. Also, exercises where members work as a group are good because the focus is on team building and working together rather than on each member specifically. Such group-building exercises include doing a building project, an art project, a ropes course, or some other experiential activity that has members working together. Leadership skill comes in processing these activities at a deeper level so members end up talking about themselves and their interaction styles.

Art activities tend to work well with many adolescents. Having members draw various pictures of things such as their home, their greatest fear, their dream, or of people having fun and then having them share their pictures often leads to sharing that can be taken to a deeper level.

For more information on working with adolescents, you may want to start with the catalog of the American Correctional Association (800-222-5646, ext. 1860). Listed in the catalog are books and videotapes on working with juveniles and youthful offenders. Two excellent resources are Jackson and Meyers (2002) and Boesky (2002).

Multicultural Populations

Correctional groups often will have a mixture of members from different ethnic, religious, and socioeconomic backgrounds. The skilled group leader plans ahead to deal with cultural differences especially among those who speak different languages or have different ways of interacting in groups due to cultural influences.

Example One: Multicultural Population

An experienced drug treatment specialist looked over her new group roster and noticed three inmates with Hispanic names. She checked with their home unit staff and discovered that two barely spoke any English so she switched a member from another group who was bilingual and had him sit near them to interpret during the group.

It is important for a correctional worker to be culturally aware to provide a beneficial working atmosphere and to make sure that members are sensitive to each other, even if they are very different. For instance, the amount of eye contact exchanged between people is interpreted differently in different cultural contexts. A group leader must anticipate and allow for different interaction patterns. When faced with persons from a different culture, the best way to learn about their culture is to talk to them and ask them directly how their behavior in the group may be affected by their culture.

Example Two: Multicultural Population

The leader meets with Kofi between the second and third group session.

Leader: Kofi, I noticed that in my group on Tuesdays you never share anything about yourself. Is it because you don't want to, don't trust the members, or don't like being in group?

Kofi: No, no. I like group. It is good. Sharing is something me not used to. In my culture, people don't tell problems.

Leader: Do you want me to keep asking you to share or would you rather me not?

Kofi: Keep asking. I thinking of sharing. I am more comfortable than first meeting.

Also, it is crucial that leaders take advantage of the many opportunities to attend classes and workshops on multicultural issues to increase their ability to work with diverse populations. There are informal ways of finding out about cultures, as well, such as discussions with other experienced coworkers. Corey (2000) has an excellent discussion on the challenges of multicultural groups and clearly states that it is the group worker's responsibility to have at least a minimal level of awareness about cultural diversity. DeLucia-Waack (1996) feels that it is important to address diversity issues within a group if those issues are hindering the effectiveness of the group.

Example Three: Multicultural Population

This group is made up of three African-Americans, one Asian, one Native American, one Iranian, and two Caucasians. It is the first session of a batterers group. It is twenty minutes into the session.

Joe: (*With a hostile, negative voice*) Speak up. None of us can hear you! Can't you look up and stop mumbling?

Leader: Wait a second, Joe. Runningdeer may have a reason for talking that way. It may be part of his culture. In this group we have people from many different cultures, and there are going to be differences in how people speak and how much eye contact people will make. My job is to try to make this comfortable for everyone. In fact, I'd like to take a couple of minutes and ask each of you to think about how your cultural upbringing may influence how you participate in this group.

In this example, the leader is aware of the cultural dimensions of the group and planned to take the time to educate them through a "mini-lecture."

Specific Group Populations Based on their Crime

Addicts

Most people working in corrections will work with addicts since many criminals have drug and/or alcohol problems. Correctional workers who lead substance abuse groups need special knowledge of addictions and they usually gain this knowledge through taking courses, attending workshops, and reading about treating those with addictions (*see* Alexander and Pratsinak, 2002). Training in cognitive-behavioral therapy is important since more and more programs are emphasizing a cognitive-behavioral approach (Latessa, 1999).

Frequently, people with no training or background in addictions are asked to lead these groups. This should not happen, because the untrained leader would not understand denial, relapse, recovery, shame, the distorted view of time, and the power of Alcoholics Anonymous (AA), and other treatment options. In this section, we briefly touch on some of the important information group leaders need to know, but we want to stress that a leader must have specific training in addictions work to be an effective addictions group leader.

Many prisons have special drug treatment programs where the inmates are involved in educational and treatment groups for up to nine months. Often leaders are supplied with purchased program material to cover in the groups. Much of the developed material is excellent, but still the first thing to assess when using purchased material is "Does this material fit with the members in this group?" Material developed may not be right for group members due to their cultural background, their intellectual level, or their life experiences. Inexperienced leaders focus primarily on delivering the material the way it is outlined. Experienced leaders give themselves permission to change the sequence of the programmed material, add some things, or omit some things to keep the members interested.

One of the hardest things about working with addicts is breaking through their denial that they have a problem. Group leaders have to know how to help members break through the distorted thinking that has them believing that their substance abuse is not a big problem, even though they are in a prison or jail in an addictions group (Twerski, 1997). Skill comes in providing a safe, caring atmosphere in the group while being able to be confrontational and allowing members to confront others about their denial. REBT and other cognitive-behavioral approaches are often the theories used to work with clients who are in denial.

Once the denial is broken, members often need to work through their shame and guilt over what they did when they were in the throes of their addiction. This is where knowledge and use of counseling theory is a must. REBT theory or some other cognitive-behavioral approach is helpful in getting them to dispute the negative self-talk that goes with their awareness of their feelings as they stay drug-free. Knowledge of support groups such as Alcoholics Anonymous (AA) and Narcotics Anonymous (NA) is also very important (Read, 1996). Recovering alcoholics and drug addicts in the community active in these groups will usually be willing to come to a prison or jail if there is enough interest in a support group. Although most institutions will emphasize a 12-Step approach using the principles of AA and NA, some institutions shy away from such programs.

Part of any addiction treatment group is relapse prevention, which deals with helping members understand what may trigger them and how important it is to have support from many sources. One important component of relapse prevention work is helping members develop a plan for their lives that does not involve using alcohol or drugs. The leader needs to make sure that the members discuss how to develop purpose and meaningful activities in their lives. In relapse prevention training, one point that is often emphasized to recovering inmates is that they should HALT. HALT is the acronym which means to never get Hungry, Angry, Lonely, or Tired. Having any of those feelings often leads to relapse. Leaders should understand the power of addiction and realize that the opportunities and temptations are minimal while in prison, but temptations are endless once the individuals are on the streets again. Inmates need a lot of help to learn how to write a new "script" for themselves that includes new people, new ways to spend time, and new ways to have fun and socialize with others.

Parks and Marlatt (1999) present an in-depth look at cognitive-behavioral approaches in their chapter "Keep 'What Works' Working: Cognitive-Behavioral Relapse Prevention Therapy with Substance Abusing Offenders." They point to numerous research projects that have had positive results using a cognitive-behavioral approach. If you are not familiar with different cognitive-behavioral approaches, we strongly encourage you to read this chapter.

In his examination of programs that are being used to treat substance abusers, Latessa (1999) outlines characteristics of an effective program and strongly challenges those working with substance abusers. He says, "When we use programs that are not effective, who gets the blame? Usually it is not the program. . . . Blaming the offender absolves us from designing and operating high-quality and effective intervention programs" (p. 237).

Sex Offenders

In federal and state prisons, groups for sex offenders are conducted because there is value in having the offenders meet as a group. Special skills and knowledge are definitely needed to lead these groups (Walsh, 2001). Group leaders need to know about helping the offenders develop a sense of "victim empathy." Leaders also need to understand the special thinking of the offenders—their need for power and control and their feelings of inadequacy. Additionally, leaders need to know how to help sex offenders deal with their shame, guilt, and the consequences of what they did. Also, leaders should be prepared to help the offenders deal with their own abuse, which is the case for most of the offenders. One important thing to do, if possible, when leading offender groups is to not call attention to the offenses by name since some prisoners will want to punish child sex abusers. When setting up these groups, rapists should not be put with pedophiles since their treatment needs are quite different.

Certainly, the goal is to make sure the members do not repeat their crime. To do this, the leader needs to focus on the triggers for the offenders, knowing that different things trigger different people. Group discussion of triggers is helpful and should be done frequently so as to get members familiar with their triggers and ways to cope when they are triggered. One creative method of dealing with this includes using guided imagery developed directly from the stories of the group members.

Example: Sex Offenders

Leader: We haven't done an imagery exercise in a while. I want to do one and get your reactions. I want you to close your eyes and see what comes up for you as I talk. (*Pause.*) I want you to imagine being at your home or apartment where you live and you are alone, flipping through channels on the television. Note the different things that come up. Some things get your attention more than others. Notice that you are getting sexually aroused by one of the things you came across so you stop and watch for a few seconds. (*Pause.*) What are you watching? You move on from that channel, but after a few seconds you go back to it. What are you feeling now? (*Pause.*) What do you do? (*Pause.*) What happens?

Eliciting their reaction and talking about alternatives is something that should be done repeatedly. Guided imagery is also used when there is denial of the trauma they have caused. Getting offenders to see the victim's experience sometimes helps to break their denial. Before leading a group of this type, leaders should do extensive reading on the subject and if at all possible attend a workshop focused specifically on working with sex offenders.

Batterers

Leaders who lack knowledge, understanding, and specific skills related to this population can easily shut down communication and create animosity between the batterer and the leader. The group leader needs knowledge and understanding of the issues that batterers face in order to create a safe space where members are willing to talk about their experiences and learn from one an other (*see* Cullen and Piekarski, 2002). The leader needs to know about anger and ways to express anger other than through hitting. Good information about the cycle of violence is essential when working with batterers. Also, the leader needs to be able to explain that physical abuse is just one form of abuse. There are many other types of abuse including verbal abuse, emotional abuse, sexual abuse, using the children, using intimidation, and using coercion and threats. Rational Emotive Behavioral Therapy (REBT) and Transactional Analysis (TA) can be very helpful by giving the members tools to understand and deal with their anger. Knowing how to teach better communication and ways to avoid fighting is a must. TA is excellent for showing the communication patterns that lead to fighting.

Since drugs and alcohol often play a major part in these offenses, the leader has to know a number of activities that address the role of drugs and alcohol in this offense. It is very important that the leader understands that this crime will be repeated unless drug and alcohol use are curtailed. For most, the use of drugs and alcohol has to stop because batterers cannot just use the drugs socially. Once they get high, then all bets are off as to how well they will control their anger.

Like sex offenders, often these inmates are worked with in groups because the group experience can help them to understand more about what they did and why they did it. Showing videotapes often helps inmates to see the buildup to the battering and see how it could be avoided. A number of tapes have been made on the subject and the better ones include good, dramatic clips of the buildup and the battering. Positive discussion can result from a ten-to-fifteen-minute film clip.

One expert, Julie L. Johnson (personal communication, 2002) said she found language to be very important. She talked about how asking "What law did you break?" is better than asking "What happened? What did you do?" According to Johnson, "asking 'What happened? What did you do?' generally leads to a long defensive story by the batterer. Asking what law they broke keeps the focus tight and on the batterer." Once the batterer identifies the law he broke, it opens the door to looking at how he reacted.

Johnson also states that during discussion, generally an offender will say "he/she made me do it; he/she pushed my buttons." This is a great opportunity to demonstrate what she calls "the button exercise." According to Johnson, the dialog would go something like this:

Example: The Button Exercise

Leader: I want you all to unbutton or button any two buttons on your shirt. (*Hopefully they have buttons; the leader waits for them to do this.*) Why did you do that?

Member: Because you told me to.

Leader: Whose buttons are those?

Member: Mine.

Leader: Who's in charge of those buttons?

Johnson states "Nine times out of ten, they begin to smile, which tells me they've connected the image and understanding. They will say something to the effect 'I own these buttons.' We discuss the idea of who really is in charge of their buttons and often I give the batterers a button to keep and use over the course of our work together as a tactile/visual reminder of being in charge of their emotional responses." This is a key component of groups of batterers—they have to accept responsibility for their behavior and learn that "no one is making them do it."

The offenders will use a lot of "she or he" statements instead of focusing on themselves. To get batterers to focus on themselves, Johnson uses journaling, reflection papers, and other writing techniques. She wants the batterers to hold themselves accountable for the role they played in the crime. For those who read and write, Johnson often has them keep a daily journal of their thoughts and also has them write papers, reflecting on what they did, how they feel about what they did, and why it was wrong. For those who are illiterate, Johnson encourages them to use pictures from magazines, make drawings, or talk into a tape recorder as a way to be in touch with their feelings and to reflect on their crime.

Johnson also does a number of creative activities using metaphors and art therapy techniques to awaken the senses of these inmates. Johnson states: "The timeline is one of the most helpful tools for me to get members to see that they could have made different choices. This visual is especially helpful when a member states 'it all happened so fast.' This is my opportunity to use the chalkboard. The timeline goes like this:

> "I draw one long line on the board with a stop at the end. The stop line represents when they hit, kicked, pushed, shoved, etc., their partner . . . or when the police arrived. I ask 'when did it stop?' The client says '8:00 p.m. The police came and I was arrested.' I then work backwards.
> "What were you doing at 7:00?"
> "We were fighting over me being late."
> "What were you doing at 6:30?"
> "I was mad 'cause she was in my face and I couldn't sleep."
> "What were you doing at 6:00?"
> "I was trying to take a nap and she kept buggin me."
> "What were you doing at 5:30?"
> "I got home and knew she was pissed and I wanted to just go take a nap."
> "What were you doing at 5:00?"
> "I was at the bar with my buddies."
> "What time did you say you would be home?"
> "About 4:00."

4:00	5:00	5:30	6:00	6:30	7:00	7:30	8:00
said I would be home	at the bar	got home	she was yelling and I wanted to take a nap	got mad she was in my face	we were fighting hollering 'cause I was late	I pushed her and told her to shut up she wouldn't and I hit her	police arrived, arrest-ed me

"Okay, let's look at this:

"We look at this timeline and the members can see how quickly the situation escalated. The members can see what started the situation and most importantly, there was a span of four hours when different choices could have been made. This is where solutions and problem solving come in by simply asking 'What could you have done differently . . . especially between 6:30 and 7:30?' Let's talk about body cues and how they can work in a situation like this."

Johnson also comments about making batterers groups multisensory and the necessity for the leader to understand the importance of early messages. She says, "I've found over the course of fifteen years or so that the majority of batterers are visual learners. Inmates use mental imaging to make sense in their world." Amen (1998) states: "The most precious treasures we have in life are the images we store in the memory banks of our brains. The sum of these stored experiences is responsible for our sense of personal identity and our sense of connectedness to those around us. Our experiences are enormously significant in making us who we are" (pp. 186-187).

Leaders have to help batterers understand how their history has much to do with their attitude about abusing others and how they have to form different images regarding hurting another person. Johnson believes that groups have to focus on this material because she contends "that if a child has recorded trauma, such as domestic violence or sexual abuse, there will be interruptions and distortions in the temporal lobe and the batterer will replay the memory/experiences while the individual is in 'relationship' with others . . . especially in stressful situations." Helping offenders work through some early childhood trauma is important in groups for batterers.

Gangs

In some prisons, gangs will be present and have to be considered when leading groups. One major decision is whether to put members from two different gangs in the same group. Sometimes the purpose of the group is to get these people to stop "warring" with each other, so they are put together. No untrained leader should lead these groups because the potential for violence is great. The leader has to be a strong person who is confident that he or she can control any group. If the purpose of the group is not for breaking down barriers between gangs but rather something else like anger management or drug treatment, then the leader always has to pay attention to the dynamics created by having members from two different gangs in the same group. The leader may have to do more educational activities since the trust level would be low.

Always the leader would be looking for ways to bridge the gap between the two gangs by using exercises that may lead to helpful discussions or even doing group-building exercises like a ropes course. If gangs are present in the group, the leader must be very conscious of what topics and exercises are chosen. For example, during the first sessions, the leader would not use dyad exercises that paired members from two different gangs. Also, the leader would not conduct trust or feedback exercises that force members to rely on the other members. Later on, these activities may work if a certain level of trust has been reached, but these should not be done during the first few sessions.

Concluding Comments

When working in corrections, group leaders will be forced to deal with various types of people and often different or specialized populations. Group members will include those who lie, are angry, quiet, uncooperative, and/or mentally challenged. Special leadership skills and understanding are needed to lead groups that focus on specific populations or specific problems.

Women face issues about being away from their children, low self-esteem, and being sexually abused as children. Getting men to share in groups is often difficult because they think it is "unmanly." Cocorrectional groups present challenges to the group leader. Groups with juveniles are often difficult because of the stage of development that adolescents are in regarding authority figures. Leading effective addictions groups is very difficult and the leader needs to know about denial, relapse, self-esteem, AA, and NA. The effective leader must be able to adjust to multicultural groups. Sex offenders and batterers groups require extra knowledge to get the members to understand themselves and learn how to prevent themselves from re-offending. Groups involving gangs are always difficult, and the leader needs to give a lot of thought to the best ways to handle gang members in groups.

Planning a Group

Planning is essential for success for most groups in a correctional setting. It is the leader's responsibility to provide an interesting and meaningful group experience. For leaders, planning means thinking through what they hope to accomplish during the entire group experience and during each session. Conscientious leaders plan the complete session: the warm-up phase, the working phase, and the closing phase. When planning, leaders need to consider the overall purpose of the group and the purpose of the specific session. Often leaders do not consider the purpose and end up with activities that are not actually relevant to the goals of the group.

Leaders have to consider the stage of the group—is it the first or second session, a middle session, or the closing session? The stage of the group often determines the type and content of exercises; that is, some exercises would not be used during the beginning stage of a group or at the closing stage. Leaders also need to consider the level of trust and commitment and the energy and attitude of the members. Additionally, leaders must give thought to how much time to spend on various activities or topics. Given all the factors to consider in order to have a session go smoothly, we strongly suggest that leaders write out a detailed plan for each session.

For groups to be effective, it is essential for the leader to have a plan even if he chooses not to follow it once the session starts. Planning a session provides a reasonably good chance that it will be meaningful. However, if the members bring up something that is relevant and the topic has lots of energy, then most likely the leader will want to go with it if it is relevant to the overall purpose. For example, the leader would most likely abandon her plan and switch to the unplanned topic of tension building in the unit if she saw that members were totally focused on some current problem to the point where they could not effectively focus on anything else. However, if the members tried to switch to a topic like what team is going to win the Super Bowl, the leader should stick to her plan and stop that discussion. The skilled leader is flexible and lives by the motto: "Stick to the plan unless something comes up that is equal to or better than the plan."

Unfortunately, many leaders in correctional settings conduct boring, meaningless sessions because they either do not see the value in planning their groups or they have no time to plan due to being assigned on the spot to lead a group because a staff member is absent or handling an emergency. We encourage all correctional workers who may be asked on the spot to lead a group in their setting to always come to work with some ideas of what they could do in a group if they were asked to lead one. Leaders who do not plan allow the members to go to whatever topic they like, which could be as superficial as complaining about the meals in the dining hall. This is an example of poor leadership. Also, some leaders who do plan, will not deviate from their plan. This, too, is a mistake. All leaders have to be flexible in order to be effective.

Planning Considerations

Warm-up Phase

The warm-up phase is the opening few minutes of a session—the time to get the members to transition from what they were doing right before coming to group to being ready to focus and share in a group setting. Often leaders make a mistake by either skipping the warm-up because a member starts talking about something or by letting the warm-up go on much longer than it should, thus causing the members to become bored. By planning the warm-up, the leader can feel confident the group will get off to a positive start. Usually what goes into the warm-up phase is checking on thoughts or reactions from the last meeting, following up on things that were discussed previously, seeing how members are feeling at the moment about being in the group, and seeing if they have anything they want to bring up for discussion.

One of the first things to consider in planning the warm-up is how much time needs to be given to this phase of the session. This varies with each group and also with the amount of time the group is meeting. If the session is an hour or less, then the leader will want to make sure the warm-up is not more than ten minutes so as to allow enough time for the middle or working phase. Part of planning the warm-up phase depends on the makeup of the members. Obviously, for a group with reluctant members, a longer warm-up will usually be necessary.

Often in the warm-up phase, the leader may ask for brief thoughts or comments since the last session or even conduct a 1-to-10 round on how the day or week has been. The leader also may ask specific people to comment on how they did in trying some new behaviors—that is, the leader may do what we call "progress reports."

Example One: Warm-up Phase

Leader: Let's start. First let's do a quick round. On a 1-to-10 scale, how was your week? 10 means "great." (*Everyone gives a number.*) Sounds like everyone had a decent week except Chuck. Would you like to talk about what made your week so bad, Chuck?

Chuck: I need to.

Leader: Okay, we'll do that in a few minutes. Before we help Chuck, Jerry, how did your phone call go with your wife?

Jerry: Much better. I stayed calm the whole time. Talking last week really helped. I kept thinking about what people said. Carlos, I did what you suggested about the note card. That really helped. I just kept staring at my notes.

Leader: Good. Jesse, how did you do with not getting so frustrated at your work detail?

Jesse: I did much better. I charted like you suggested and it never got above a 5. One time it started to and I remember what Phil had said about counting to 10 and thinking about something else. That really did help.

Note that in this example, by using the strategy of checking with each member during the warm-up phase, the leader does not get stuck on Chuck.

Often the leader will conduct a "yes/no" round to see if members have something they want to bring up in group. This is a very quick way to find out who wants some "air time" during the session.

Example Two: Warm-up Phase

Leader: The plan is to continue talking about trust, but before we do that, I want to see if anyone has something they want to bring up. We'll do a "yes/no" round. Let's start with you, Jill.

Jill: There's nothing special on my mind.

Kirsten: No.

Anita: Maybe

Vicki: Yes.

Candy: No

Rigel: Yes

Leader: Briefly, Rigel and Vicki, what were your "yeses?"

In this example, the leader uses a "yes/no" round to decide where to start. Another good opening round right at the start of the group is the "here/getting here/ not here" round where the leader asks each member to say one of the three phrases regarding their readiness to start the group. This helps the leader to judge how quickly he should move to the middle phase.

Example Three: Warm-up Phase

Leader: Okay, let's get started. Let's start with a round of either "here," "getting here," or "not here," referring to if you are mentally here and ready to focus on group.

Josh: Here.

Richard: Here.

Winston: Getting here.

Dick: Not here.

Dave: Mostly here.

Leader: Dick, anything we can do to help you get here?

Dick: I'm still pissed off about what happened a few minutes ago. I think I am going to get written up.

Leader: Do you want to take a few minutes and talk about it now or would you rather do it after group?

Dick: I thought you wanted to show a film.

Leader: We have time.

In this example, the "here/getting here/not here" here round identified the members who early on need to work. By planning the warm-up phase, the leader knows what he will be doing and has reasonable confidence that the warm-up will be interesting. Far too often, leaders open with a boring, irrelevant warm-up phase and then wonder why the group is so hard to lead.

Middle/Working Phase

Planning the middle phase is essential because otherwise it is merely left up to chance whether something meaningful will happen. Too often, leaders think they have planned when all they have done is think of a topic and an activity. Planning includes giving careful thought to what activities or topics would be relevant and meaningful, and what questions and points need to be covered. This is where knowing the "ins and outs" of a topic and having a human behavior theory come into play. Common mistakes in planning the working phase include:

- Not planning
- Planning unrelated topics or activities
- Planning too much so that there is no time for anything meaningful
- Not allowing enough time to process exercises
- Planning superficial discussions and activities instead of planning discussions that will take the group to a deeper, more meaningful level

In the classes we teach on group counseling, students at first find it difficult to write good middle phase plans, but after some practice and feedback most are able to do this quite well. It does take practice and careful thought.

Closing Phase

Planning the closing phase of a group is important because so often when it is not planned, leaders skip the closing because they did not pay enough attention to their time. Having a closing is very important and leaders will want to think about how they want to close each session. Often a closing round of what stood out is all that is needed, but sometimes leaders may want to have members write down what stood out or share in dyads what has been important. Also, the leader will want to allow at least five minutes for closing to bring the group to an end. Many times leaders who do not plan for a closing run out of time and just abruptly stop the group. This is not good planning.

Back-up Plan

Leaders will always want to have a back-up plan in case an exercise does not work or a topic does not generate the energy expected. Too often, leaders have one activity or one topic planned, and if the members do not like it, those leaders are lost because they do not have an alternative plan. Skilled leaders anticipate that some things will "bomb" or "run out of steam" so they are ready with some other interesting subjects or exercises.

Planning for Changes in Group Membership

New Members Joining the Group

Many groups in correctional settings are "open groups." An open group is one that has new members coming into the group periodically or sometimes in nearly every session. The leader of an open group always should plan how to introduce the new member to the group. The biggest mistake we see with introduction of a new member is to focus too much time on the new member by going over all the group rules and reviewing much of what has taken place previously. Some leaders also make the mistake of having the new member spend a rather long time introducing himself or herself. Our suggestion is to have brief introductions of the other members and of the new member and then go on with the group, letting the new member come up to speed as the group moves along. One technique that works well is to have each member say his name and one thing that stands out to him about the group or one thing which he is working to change. This serves the purpose of a warm-up and also helps the new member learn something about the group and about each member. After this round, the leader gives the new member a chance to speak but does not force him to do so. Throughout the session and at the closing, the leader should observe how the new member seems to be adjusting to being in the group and should try to draw him out during the session and at the closing. The key is to not bore the current members by focusing on the new member—the focus should be on making the group interesting for the old members.

Members Absent from the Group

In correctional groups, at times a member will be absent due to some violation. In probation and parole groups, a member may be absent because of a probation or parole violation and may have been sent to jail or prison. In prisons, a person may be in isolation due to some infraction of prison policy. When this happens, the leader may want to plan as part of the working phase of the session a discussion on what has happened to the member since the other members most likely will be aware of and/or upset about what has happened to the member.

Members Leaving the Group

In open groups, not only do new members join the group, but also members leave to go to other institutions or home. Usually the leader knows ahead of time that a member will be leaving, but at times this comes up on the day of the group, so leaders always should plan for the possibility of needing to say good-bye to a departing member. Depending on the member and how well other members know this individual, this may take anywhere from three minutes to as long as fifteen minutes. For members who have worked hard in the group, and when members know the departing member fairly well, allowing as much as fifteen minutes is not uncommon.

With departing members, some of the possible things to cover include:

- What they have learned
- What their plan is for staying out of trouble
- How they could lose what they have gained in the group

- Their plan for establishing a support system
- Their strengths

There are many options as to when to say good-bye to a departing member. Many leaders focus on saying good-bye to a departing member right before starting the closing phase. Some leaders close the group, then do the good-bye for the departing member. Some leaders prefer to do the good-bye in the beginning. Usually this depends on the group and the member who is leaving. The important point is that this should be a planned activity that fits into the scheme for the whole session.

Sample Plans

In this section, we present five plans. By showing these different plans, we hope you will gain a clear idea of the thought that goes into planning. When reading these plans, you will want to pay attention to:

- The flow of the plan
- The timing of things
- The three phases—the opening, the middle, and the closing

Do not worry if you are not familiar with terms or concepts, since the primary focus is on how to plan. We believe that writing plans in the way shown, with the times in the margin, is helpful. Also, plans written this way are easy to use during the session itself. We encourage leaders to take their plan into the session and glance at it for guidance.

Plan One

This is the first of three sessions of an adjusting-to-prison-life group.

Purpose of the session: Warm-up to the group process, interest members in the topic, introduce REBT.

WARM-UP PHASE

3 min. Introductions-round (name, where from, how long of a sentence; also introduce self).

15 min. Discuss the group—format, purpose (stress that it is mainly an educational and support group and not a therapy group). Have members share their needs and any fears or questions about the group. Have them share cultural differences. Use the following sentences to facilitate discussion.

1. When I enter a new group, I feel_______________.
2. When people first meet me, they_______________.
3. In a group, I am most afraid of_______________.
4. In a group, I feel annoyed when the leader_______________.

(Sandwich in the group rules of confidentiality, attendance, no attacking others, use of eyes, and the need for cutting off.)

MIDDLE/WORKING PHASE

2 min. Complete the following sentences.

1. The hardest thing about being in prison is_______________.
2. I get most upset while being here when _______________.
3. One positive thing about being in prison is_______________.

30 min. Have members share answers to the first two sentences and discuss ways to cope. Teach them REBT—thoughts cause your feelings.

10 min. Discuss question on focusing on ways to use their time in prison to benefit them.

20 min. Discuss attitudes and how they can change theirs—continue to use REBT.

5 min. Triads—discuss what stood out.

CLOSING PHASE

5 min. Share what stood out, feelings about the group, one thing they plan to do differently. Remind them of the next meeting time.

In the sample plan, the leader made sure that the purpose was clearly stated, that each phase was planned, and that there were structured activities appropriate for a first group.

One noticeable feature of this plan is the estimated number of minutes for each activity. (Some find it easier to write in the projected times, such as 2:00, 2:10, and so forth.) This is important so that leaders have a general idea of about how long they want to spend on any portion of the plan. Leaders should never stick rigidly to the estimates, but having the estimated times helps to prevent staying too long on an activity, especially when the activity is not being that beneficial. There will be many times when it is better for the group to stay longer with an activity, and by having the estimated times, the leader can quickly look through her plan and see what she will need to cut out.

In any first session, leaders want to have a plan for how to start the group. In Chapter 12, we discuss in great detail how to begin a group, so here we simply want to point out that the first eighteen minutes of the above plan is for warm-up and informing the members about what to expect in the group. This is a rather long warm-up phase, but often first sessions require more time for warming up the members. The sentence completion serves as a way to focus the members on the group and how they are feeling about being in the group. As we said earlier, sentence completion is always a helpful way to get members to talk. Also note that the plan does not call for covering the group rules during the first couple of minutes, nor is there a five-minute segment for covering the rules. Instead, the plan calls for mentioning the rules during the discussion of the different sentence completions. It is usually better to cover the rules this way than to have a long, boring discussion about "group rules."

To get into the purpose of the group, the plan calls for the members to complete a second set of three sentences regarding their feelings about being in prison. Also note that teaching the theory of REBT is planned. This theory is chosen since it deals directly with how one's thoughts cause one's feelings, and the purpose of the group is, in part, to deal with their feelings about being in prison. To vary the format, the leader uses triads as another way to get members to share. Dyads and triads often are good activities because some members feel uncomfortable talking in the large group but will talk when there are only one or two other people. The plan ends with a five-minute closing consisting of a round of what stood out and a discussion of what members plan to do differently.

Plan Two

This is the second session of a counseling/therapy group. Since many of the members seem to be having trouble making friends, the leader has planned this session on that topic. There is one new member this week.

Purpose of the session: Continue warming members up to the group process, introduce the new member, focus on the topic of stroke economy.

WARM-UP PHASE

5 min. For new member, have members tell their names and what they remember about last week. Have new member comment about being in the group and being in prison.

5 min. Ask for comments, reactions, or thoughts about the week and last week's session. Comment about the group and its purpose. Also, remind members when they talk to look at others instead of the leader.

MIDDLE/WORKING PHASE

10 min. Stroke economy exercise before prison.

10 min. Stroke economy exercise here at the prison—each person does his own. Process thoughts and feelings about their current economy.

2 min. Have members list things they can do to improve their economy.

5 min. Discuss lists in triads.

20 min. List ideas on chalkboard. Discuss the ideas. Role-play some of the ideas. Have each member practice or comment on what he is going to do this week.

CLOSING PHASE

3 min. Summarize—each member completes "One thing I learned today in group is . . ."

In this plan, the leader knows there is going to be a new member, which often happens in prison groups, so she plans how to integrate the new member into the group. The next part of the warm-up phase consists of asking for comments or reactions from last week. Once the leader feels the group is warmed up, she plans to conduct the stroke economy exercise (*see* Chapter 8 for a detailed explanation of the exercise). The leader plans to spend less time on the stroke economy before prison because her goal is to get members to look at their current stroke economy and see how they can change it. The leader plans to use a number of activities to get members to focus on improving their current stroke economies. She plans to use writing, discussing in triads, and discussing ideas in the large group. A brief, three-minute closing is planned for the end.

Plan Three

This is the third session of a weekly therapy group for inmates. The group has six members.

Purpose of the session: Focus on negative aspects of drugs, identify and challenge self-talk about drugs.

WARM-UP PHASE

5 min. Any thoughts from the week or from the last session?

MIDDLE/WORKING PHASE

4 min. Make a list of:

- Five things I liked about using/selling drugs and alcohol
- Five things I did not like about using/selling drugs and alcohol

4 min. Focus on the five things they liked.

10 min. Focus on the five things they did not like. Expect answers such as:

- Prison
- People being angry with them
- People being hurt
- Destroyed relationships
- Fights
- Pain
- Fear

10 min. Discuss self-talk about use of drugs and alcohol. Expect the following:

- Low Frustration Tolerance—I can't stand it.
- This is who I am.
- I have to be this way.
- I must have lots of money to be happy or to be respected.

20 min. Teach REBT—thoughts cause feelings, and challenge self-talk.

CLOSING PHASE

3 min. Round—what stood out?

4 min. Write in journals (Journals are left for the leader to read).

In Plan Three, a brief warm-up is followed by a written activity that will most likely engage most of the members. The leader plans to focus briefly on the positive aspects of using and dealing drugs since the purpose is to get them to see the negative aspects of using and selling drugs. Ten minutes is spent on getting them to identify their self-talk about their use of drugs and alcohol. Next is the teaching and discussion of REBT and how members can challenge their self-talk. (This theory or another cognitive-behavior theory would be used in the remaining sessions to dispute the negative and self-defeating self-talk that members bring up.) For the closing, the leader uses a round and then asks the members to write any reactions in their journal. Journal writing sometimes serves as a way for members to share more with the leader and is an activity that leaders should consider for most therapy groups. Many inmates write very little but some may write very revealing thoughts and feelings that they did not want to share in the group.

Plan Four

This plan is for a unit meeting with twenty inmates.

Purpose of the session: Discuss improving the social climate on the unit because many have complained about how tense and uncomfortable it is living there.

WARM-UP PHASE

5 min. Announcements: schedule changes; phone privileges and use; new rules regarding Sunday visitation.

5 min. "Yes/no" round if they have something they want to bring up. If yes, find out what the yeses are and then either focus on them or tell the person or persons you will talk with them after the meeting.

MIDDLE/WORKING PHASE

10 min. Focus on yeses or go to exercise.

2 min. Round 1-to-10 with 10 being as good as possible, rate the climate on the unit.

10 min. Bring half the inmates to the middle—discuss "What do you see as the reason why there is not a good climate on the unit?" Try to get them talking about yelling, complaining, lack of consideration, and so forth. Have people on the outside of the circle listen and think about what can be done.

10 min. Bring other half to the center; discuss what can be done.

3 min. If discussion has gone well, have each list what they are willing to do differently.

10 min. Discuss in triads (groups of three) their list.

15 min. Discuss in whole group changes they are willing to make.

I could have them write anonymously one thing they are willing to do and one thing they wish someone else would do and read them to the group; this would generate discussion.

CLOSING PHASE

5 min. Review the announcements and major points. Ask some to comment on what stood out.

Plan Four starts with announcements and a "yes/no" round to see if any member has anything he wants to bring up. The plan allows for time to focus on the yeses but also has activities in case no one has anything to bring up. The leader plans a round to focus members on the topic, which is the poor social climate on the unit. Since the group is so large, the leader plans to use the inner/outer circle strategy as a way to get members to share—often members will share if the group seems smaller. In hopes of keeping members focused on improving the social climate, the leader plans a listing activity followed by triads. The leader will spend the last fifteen minutes of the working phase discussing what members have been thinking about and saying in their triads. The closing is a review of the important things that have been discussed. The leader will get some members to comment on what stood out but does not plan a complete round because of the size of the group.

Plan Five

This plan is for a task group for screening and sorting inmates for groups starting in two weeks. The eight members are correctional officers, caseworkers, and work supervisors.

Purpose of the session: To screen members for groups.

WARM-UP PHASE

5 min. Tell about each group (anger, prison adjustment, or personal awareness); also have a handout with each described.

5 min. Questions about the purpose of each of the groups.

WORKING PHASE

5 min. List inmates you think need the groups and who would be good members. Also, list inmates who need the groups but may not be such good members.

25 min. Go over the list.

10 min. Ask, "What other groups would you like to see started?"

8 min. Have group make comments about the groups and how they could be better.

CLOSING PHASE

2 min. Summarize/review the plan for handling the questionable situations; thank them for coming.

The plan calls for a warm-up phase that is straightforward—discuss the purpose and get started as quickly as possible. By planning the working phase, the leader knows exactly what she wants to accomplish during the one-hour meeting. The plan for the closing is fine because it serves as a reminder to the leader to review what was decided about those in question.

Other Planning Considerations

Along with the planning of a session, the leader has other planning responsibilities. The leader has to plan the best time of day for the group to meet. Unfortunately, in many settings, there are no options, but when there is a choice, the leader will want to try to figure out when would be the best time to meet. Too, if you find that the time planned for the group is not a good one, you may want to talk with the administration about changing the schedule so as to maximize the chance for the group to be successful.

Another planning consideration is how often the group should meet. Each group is different. Some groups meet daily, some twice a week, and some once a week. As the leader, you will want to figure out what seems to be best for the type of group and the commitment level of the members. Often, this is not the leader's choice as the prison schedule dictates the frequency of meetings. In some settings, groups meet too often, and in other settings, groups do not meet often enough. If necessary, you will want to try to influence the administration to have groups meet the optimal number of times rather than have the frequency be dictated by a general policy of the institution.

Concluding Comments

Good planning leads to funneling and therefore, impact. The skilled leader always plans the warm-up, realizing that the opening few minutes of any session are very important. The warm-up should be relevant, never boring, nor too long. The plan for the middle or working phase should be in line with the purpose of the session. There should always be a plan for the closing phase—groups should not end abruptly. The prepared leader also should have a back-up plan in case what is planned does not work. Leaders of open groups plan for new members, absent members, and for members to depart the group. Other planning considerations include planning the meeting time and the number of meetings per week. As we said throughout the chapter, planning is very important; yet, we find that close to half the group leaders in correctional settings do not spend adequate time planning their groups.

Starting Groups

The first session of a group is very important because it often sets the tone for the entire life of the group (Gladding, 2003). The first session should be more than just a warm-up session filled mainly with introductions, group rules, and information about the purpose of the group. Meaningful content needs to be discussed during some portion of the first session. Given its importance, there are many different things to think about when planning and conducting a first session. Often leaders do not give enough thought to or do not know what is important to cover in the first session. Since the initial session is so important, leaders should spend extra time planning to ensure that the session will be interesting and inviting instead of boring and negative. Consideration should be given to each of the following:

- The opening minutes
- How to introduce yourself
- How to have members introduce themselves
- Setting a positive, working tone/using voice
- How to explain the purpose of the group
- Explaining how the group will be conducted
- Focusing some of the time on meaningful discussion
- Telling members about how you will be looking around
- Telling members about how you may have to interrupt and cut off at times
- How you will cover the group rules
- Drawing out members, if necessary
- Cutting off members, if necessary
- How members are feeling about the group
- The closing of the session

The Opening Minutes

The opening minutes of the first session are important and leaders always should consider how to start the group in an interesting way. Usually introductions are conducted along with some discussion about the purpose of the group and the group rules. In some groups, leaders may see the need to start with something more dramatic or unique to get members' attention. For instance, in an anger management group, the leader may start by staging being very angry with a member (all set up ahead of time) just to get the members' attention. In a case like this, the leader would use the anger outburst as an example of how anger needs to be managed. Our message is ***feel free to be creative***! Leaders who do not understand the importance of the opening minutes let the introduction and first few minutes unfold in a rather unexciting manner, setting a boring or negative tone for the group.

Introductions

One of the first things that occurs in most groups is the introduction of members, which should be meaningful, interesting, and relevant. Usually the leader will want to do some type of introduction of herself and also of the members. Naturally, if the members know each other, the introduction can be skipped or greatly shortened. A common mistake is for leaders to have members give long, boring introductions where each member talks for two-to-five minutes. This takes most of the time allotted for the first session and does not tend to build any feeling of being in a group. In most first sessions, the leader should keep the introductions to no more than one minute; usually thirty seconds per person is plenty of time for relevant information to be shared. Too, it is important to make sure that what the members are sharing is relevant and interesting for the others to hear. For example, all the places they have lived or the names of all the prisons they have been in is information that is not relevant to the group.

Example: Bad Introduction

Leader: (*With a flat, unenergetic voice*) This group will be about managing anger. Everyone needs to manage anger, especially here since we are overcrowded by 30 percent. We are supposed to have only 1,000 inmates, but we have 1,300. They say the reason is lack of funds and more drug arrests. I am Donnie Davis. I have been working at the prison for twelve years, ever since it opened. No, actually it has now been thirteen years. My wife also works here. I grew up in this area. I worked at the county jail before working here at the prison. My main hobby is hunting. This first session is going to be a get-to-know-you session. Who would like to introduce himself?

Felix: I will. I am Felix Jones. I have been here three years. I have been in prison for the last ten years. I was in a prison in California and one in Texas before being here. My wife is in California so she does not get to visit very often and she only writes about once every two weeks. My sister writes me more than my wife. My sister thinks my wife is seeing someone else. I never developed any hobbies because I have been dealing drugs since I was twelve.

Jerome: I have been dealing drugs since I was ten.

Billy: Felix, where in California did you live? I grew up in the Bay Area.

Felix: L.A., mostly.

Clay: Where in L.A.? I lived there for a few years.

In this example, the leader did not model what he was really wanting. He had no energy in his voice and he provided lots of irrelevant information. The members modeled their introduction after his. The introduction round went astray with the members talking about irrelevant things. Some leaders do not pay attention to how they start their groups, and therefore their first sessions get off course and end up being boring or about subjects not relevant to the purpose. The opening introduction and first few minutes usually are a good indication of how the entire group will go, and the leader should do all that is possible to make sure the group gets off to a good start.

Example: Good Introduction

Leader: (*With a strong, energized voice*) Let's get started. As you know, this is a group on anger management, which I think is a very relevant topic for many here in the prison. In talking with you, I know that many of you expressed a desire to manage your anger better. We'll get into that in just a few minutes. First, I would like to have each of you introduce yourself since many of you do not know each other. Simply say your name and one situation where your anger gets away from you. I'll start. I am Donnie Davis, and if I am not careful I can get angry when I come to work here and find that I am going to have to fill in on another unit.

Felix: I am Felix. I have been here three years. I have been in prison . . .

Leader: (*With a calm, kind voice*) Felix, let me interrupt. For now, let's just do your name and one situation where you get angry.

Felix: Okay. I am Felix, and I get angry when people get into my stuff.

Jerome: I am Jerome. I get angry at mealtime when they give me such small portions.

In this example, the leader used his voice and modeled what should be said in the round. He stopped Felix from getting off track and he made the introduction round relevant to the purpose of the group. Also, the leader set a tone that this was serious by commenting that they would be getting into anger management techniques sometime during the first session.

Use of Voice/Setting the Tone

One element in making the group positive and inviting is the leader's voice. A lively voice can help set an encouraging tone. A positive, upbeat voice can energize the inmates, which is quite useful since the members are often not interested in being in a group. It is up to the leader to set the tone in the group. Remember, the members are cuing off your energy so you will want to have an energetic voice when conducting the first session. As a leader, you will always want to be aware of what type of tone you want to set, and most of the time you want a positive, friendly, supportive tone so that members feel safe and will share. It is also important to realize that other members can set a negative tone if the leader is not paying attention. Members can attack each other, be very silly, or be very negative. During the first few sessions, the leader will want to make sure that members do not influence the tone of the group in a negative way.

Leaders often make two mistakes about the tone. One mistake is setting a very relaxed, nonserious tone. This leads to sessions where nothing meaningful is accomplished because the message has been sent that not much is going to happen, that we're just here to fill time. The other mistake occurs when leaders set a very hard, harsh tone that sounds almost militaristic. The leader comes on like a dictator or taskmaster. This turns members off and they tune out the leader and the group.

The Purpose of the Group and How it Will Be Conducted

It is important during the session to spend some time explaining the purpose of the group and how it will be conducted. Leaders often use an activity such as a sentence completion that focuses on the purpose of the group, or they simply spend a couple of minutes discussing why the group is meeting and how it will be conducted. Leaders explain their role, how active they will be, the role of the members, the types of activities, and the purpose of the group. Sometime during the first session, leaders also should tell the members that they will be looking around or "scanning" and not just focusing on the person talking. Leaders also need to explain that there will be times when they will need to interrupt members and redirect the discussion. It is important to cover these two points during the first session; otherwise, the members may be confused when the leader is not looking at the person talking or may become hostile when the leader interrupts a member.

Example: How the Group Will Be Conducted

About three minutes into the first group session, the leader is asked about how the group is going to be run.

Member: What do we do here? Sit around and talk, or do we have to listen to you or what?

Leader: As you know, this is a drug education group so that means we'll cover various topics about drugs. It's a group, so that means you'll be talking. In fact, I would say that I'll be talking or showing a video or having a speaker for about a third or half of each session, and then I'll facilitate your talking, reacting, or asking questions during the remaining time. In other words, you can't just come and sit. I'll have you do various activities and get reactions or responses to those activities. When sharing, I will make sure no one is attacked for his responses, and I'll try to get some of you to talk more and probably get some of you to talk less. Two things I did want to mention. First, when you are talking, there will be times when I will be looking at other members and not at you. I do this because I am trying to get a sense of how others are reacting to what you are saying. When you are talking, the tendency is that you will look only at me and I want you to look at others so let my looking around serve as a signal to you to look around. Second, as I said, I will be trying to draw some of you out, and also I may have to cut some of you off. If I cut you off, it is because I see that others want to talk or that we need to move on, or that perhaps you have gotten off the subject. In other words, it is my responsibility to make sure no one dominates and that we stay on track. For those of you who tend to not talk, I will gently encourage you to say things. No one has to say a lot, but I will be asking each of you to share some.

Expectations of Members

Since most inmates do not really want to be in a group, many have not given any thought as to how a group can be helpful, so it is usually best not to ask members what they expect from the group. In later sessions and in some first sessions of treatment groups, a discussion of expectations can be valuable, but we strongly suggest that you not ask for expectations unless you see that the members seem to have some energy for the topic. Certainly, for task groups and for groups with staff, a discussion of expectations during the first session would be very appropriate.

Addressing Confidentiality and Other Group Rules

Some leaders make the mistake of spending too much time on group rules, which usually is boring. The rules can be covered quite briefly. Most members understand that they cannot attack other members and that only one person should talk at a time. For certain groups, a discussion about confidentiality will be necessary because members are concerned about what the leader is going to tell other staff members and what members are going to tell others outside the group. Most group members understand the importance of confidentiality, but for some groups it may be impossible to get members to be confidential. In that case the leader has to modify how she is going to conduct the group since the members would not be willing to share on a personal level.

As for what members should and should not say in group, the leader has to be clear as to what she has to report to the administration so that members can choose whether or not to disclose information. The leader can say something like the following:

"I will maintain confidentiality concerning what you do and say in these sessions as long as you do not hurt or threaten to hurt yourself or anyone else and do not discuss unsolved crimes or escape plans" (Van Voorhis, Braswell, and Lester, 2000; p. 51).

Using Interesting Exercises/Focusing on Meaningful Discussion

During the first session, it is important to pick exercises that are interesting and will cause members to listen to what others have to say. Members usually are curious about how others answered the same questions that they were asked to answer. Leaders should always ask themselves if what they have planned is going to be of interest to those in their group, knowing that the members may be negative and disinterested. If the opening few minutes of the first session are boring, there is a good chance that the members will lose focus and the leader will have to work very hard to engage them in meaningful discussions. The key is for the leader to make sure that what he has planned is engaging.

In Chapter 8, we discussed exercises that are excellent to consider using for the first session. Many of these creative activities can be used to stimulate curiosity and interest. Rounds and written and movement exercises are excellent ways to keep members involved. We have found that the more comfortable leaders get with choosing and leading exercises, the more appealing and interesting they make the first sessions.

Dominating Members

In the first session, leaders set the tone for the entire series of sessions. Thus, leaders want to make sure that members have some expectation that they will be given a chance to talk. Often in first sessions, leaders make the mistake of allowing one member to dominate the group either because the leader is happy someone is talking or the leader is not comfortable using cut-off skills. By letting a member dominate, an antitherapeutic tone is established. That is, the other members get the feeling that one member will do most of the talking and they do not have to say much. Also, members may be frustrated with the leader because they want to talk but the dominating member always brings the focus back to himself. It is important not to "sacrifice" the group in order to be nice to one member, especially during the first session when the tone for the entire group is being set.

Drawing Out

During the first session, it is very important for the leader to try to get each member to share at different times during the session. The reason for this is to get members used to the idea that there is some expectation that they will talk during the group meetings. Given the correctional population, some members will be hesitant to speak, thus putting more responsibility on the leader to have various strategies for getting members to share. As we said earlier, the best way to get members to talk is to use interesting activities and topics. Still, members will be hesitant, especially during a first session when they are feeling uncomfortable and have no sense of trust. The leader needs to give much thought to how to draw out the quiet members during the first session. We suggest written exercises, rounds, and movement exercises (*see* Chapter 8).

How Members Feel about Being in the Group

During the first session, leaders should pay close attention to how the members seem to be feeling about being in the group. Leaders want to observe if members seem comfortable or uncomfortable, eager or hesitant cooperative or uncooperative. These observations can help the leader to adjust the plan to fit the members during the first session. Having comfortable, eager, cooperative members would be quite different from having uncomfortable, hesitant, uncooperative members. In most first sessions, the leader does not want to go too deeply into things, but should do more with eager, cooperative members. Leaders who do not see that members are ready and eager to go deeper often spend more time than necessary doing ice-breaker activities where they really could be getting into valuable and meaningful content. On the other hand, some leaders make the mistake of moving too quickly into content areas while the members are still hesitant and need more warm-up time. The key is to pay attention to the members. If need be, ask them about their comfort level and if they are ready to go deeper into some issues.

Closing the Session

The closing phase of the first session is important because the leader will want to hear reactions to the session. Often, the leader will want to take some time to summarize what happened during the session and discuss possible topics and activities for future sessions. The leader should allow some extra time in closing the first session to discuss any issues about the group since some members may have questions about why certain things happened. The leader needs to be prepared for members to comment on what they did not like about the group or how it was different from other prison groups in which they have been. This is especially true when the leader is active and tries to focus the group using theories and exercises and the members have been in groups where the leader did very little and the members discussed whatever they wanted. In Chapter 13, we discuss further the closing phase of a group.

Second Session

Second sessions are still part of getting the group headed in the right direction and can be problematic or catch leaders off guard. If the first session went well, some leaders relax and expect that the members will carry on in the second session as they did in the first session. Sometimes this happens and sometimes it does not. Sometimes the members do not have the same energy that they had for the first session and the leader is caught off guard. Leaders always need to have a solid plan for the second session and anticipate that the members will be less talkative. On the other hand, if the first session went poorly, the leader will want to evaluate as best he can what went wrong and try to change it. The leader would want to make certain that what is planned is interesting and engaging since the members already would have a negative mindset as a result of the first session.

Concluding Comments

The group leader must do much planning for the first session of any group since the tone is usually set during that session. The leader should plan how he wants to introduce himself and how he wants the members to introduce themselves. Also, the leader needs to make sure that the opening minutes are not boring and that some relevant content is discussed. The leader needs to pay attention to the tone of her voice that would be most effective for the session. During the session, the leader needs to discuss briefly the group rules, issues of confidentiality, how the group will be conducted, how he will be looking around, and how he may be cutting off and drawing out members. During the session, the leader should observe how the members are feeling about being in a group and make sure no one dominates the session. The leader needs to give thought to the closing of the first session and the second session, since it is also important for setting the tone for the remainder of the sessions.

[illegible] during the session the leader needs to dis-
[illegible] the group may [illegible]
[illegible] and how he may be getting
[illegible] the leader should
[illegible] members [illegible] in a group [illegible]
[illegible] the session the leader [illegible] brought
the closing [illegible] and the second session, [illegible]
[illegible] of the session.

Closing a Session and Closing the Group

As we said earlier, there are three phases to a session: the warm-up, the middle, and the closing. The closing phase is the time when the leader ties the entire session together, gets members to share their thoughts and feelings, and brings the session to a close. Leaders need to plan how they are going to conduct the closing phase because if they do not, they often do a quick closing, or even worse, run out of time and have no closing whatsoever. Some groups meet for a designated time, and the leader who does not plan for the closing may get so caught up that time simply runs out and the members have to go to their next activity, catch the bus, or go to work.

Time Allotted for Closing

The closing phase usually lasts between three and ten minutes, depending on the length of the session, the type of group, the topics discussed, and the interactions that have taken place. The leader should allow some extra time for closing the first session to discuss any issues about the group that members may have. In sessions where there was heavy, emotional work or tense interactions, the leader should allow extra time for closing.

What to Cover

Usually the closing phase should consist of some type of summary of what happened, especially in task, education, and discussion groups. Either the leader does the summarizing or the group as a whole summarizes what stood out or what got accomplished. With therapy groups, the leader should make sure there is no unfinished business or at least make sure the members are not too emotionally upset. In groups that go to deeper levels of work, it is very important that the leader allow enough time to bring the members back up mentally and emotionally so that they can leave the group and go to the next scheduled activity, be it a meal, work, or recreation. The leader who fails to allow time for members to "decompress" is really not being sensitive to the prison situation where people do not have a choice as to what they do next. Inmates often do not have the time to "collect" themselves, so it is the leader's task to provide for this during the closing phase.

In many groups, leaders use the closing phase as a time for members to discuss what they learned, possibly what they did not like about the session, and what they would like to see in future sessions. Feedback about the group or even feedback to other members may be done during the closing phase.

New Topics

New topics should not be covered during the closing. It is common for members to wait until the end to bring up major or personal issues. If faced with this problem, leaders can handle it by discussing with members the fact that they are doing this. The leader can say while there is plenty of time left something like, "Does anyone have anything major they want to bring up while there still is plenty of time? Please, don't wait until the last ten minutes." If something does come up when there is not enough time to handle it, the leader simply needs to say something like:

> **Leader:** Let's hold that subject until another session because it will take too long. We need to spend the next five minutes or so winding down from today's session. Any more thoughts or reactions to what we did here today?

Or if an inmate is still emotionally upset and needs to talk, the leader could say:

> **Leader:** Sherry, we need to close so we can't talk about that right now. When we finish, let's you and I talk and I'll see if I can help you or get you to someone who can.

How to Begin the Closing Phase

It is the leader's responsibility to watch the clock in order to allow for enough time to close the session. The leader usually tells the members that it is time to start winding down. The leader can start the closing by saying either of the following:

- "Let's take the next few minutes to summarize and close the session."
- "I want us to begin closing for the day. I want you to think about what

you learned today and one thing you are going to do differently. I'd like to hear from each of you."

Example: Beginning the Closing

Leader: We are going to start winding down. I'd like each of you to think of what you are going to take away from the session. Think of at least two things you are thinking about as a result of the group today. Who wants to go first?

Mary: I am definitely going to think about the Critical Parent in me. That really hit home, as did the part about not nurturing yourself. I am going to try to nurture myself more.

Lindy: That's what stands out to me too! I am so critical. I am going to try this Sunday to be nice to my family when they come to visit. I really liked acting out some of those visiting scenes.

Leader: That's great. I hope all of you really think about ways to nurture yourself. Next meeting I am going to ask you about how you have been nurturing yourself.

Exercises to Use in Closing

Writing

To start the closing phase, the leader may want to first have the members list things that they learned or new ideas that stood out. By having them write something out, the members get to organize their thoughts and it makes it easier for the leader to call on them. Another writing activity that some leaders use at the very end of the session is to have the members take as much time as they want to write in their journal any reactions or thoughts they have as a result of the session. This would come after a few minutes of closing when people have said what they want to say. The leader would hand out journals in which members write. Some members are anxious to leave and will only write a sentence. Other members write a page or two, revealing things in writing that they did not want to share during the session. The members leave the journals for the leader to read, and the leader either gives them back the next day or at the next session. For some members, this serves as a good way for them to communicate their feelings to the leader. It also helps the leader to understand what is going on in some of the members' minds since members often do not reveal very personal thoughts and feelings in the group.

Rounds

One of the best activities to use for closing is the round because it gives everyone a chance to speak. As in the example above, the leader may ask for a word or phrase or a brief comment about what stood out. During the round, the leader often emphasizes some point that a person is making, as in the example below, where a closing round is taking place and Ginny makes a comment which the leader chooses to explore further.

Example: Emphasizing a Point in a Closing Round

Leader: Ginny, what did you learn today?

Ginny: I learned that I don't have to hate my parents.

Leader: That is so right. None of you has to hate your parents and hate takes up energy and time. As we said, most of you had parents who did not do the best job in the world, but now you are all young adults and it is your job to make your life work. None of you live with your parents and probably never will. Next week I want to talk more about this. Others of you, what did you learn?

Ellie: I learned that I am a lot like my mother, and I want to work hard to change that.

A round also can be used to rate on a 1-to-10 scale how valuable the session was, or even to rate various aspects of the session, such as the video, the reading, or the exercise. This type of feedback is especially helpful if the leader plans to lead the same group in the future. A round regarding what each member is going to do differently is valuable in many treatment groups. This type of round gets members to commit aloud to some behavioral change they are going to implement before the next group session.

Dyads

If a lot has happened during the session and the leader wants to make sure members get a chance to say things aloud, he can use dyads. The leader can pair the members up or let them pick a partner and then have them share what has stood out to them during the session. The value of this is that the members get to share thoughts and feelings with at least one other person for a few minutes. Dyads allow for everyone to get to share many thoughts and feelings, whereas in the large group, the leader has to keep the sharing to a minimum; otherwise, the closing can last twenty to twenty-five minutes, which, in many groups, is close to half the time.

Example: Using Dyads to Begin the Closing

Leader: We have about ten minutes left, and I want to take some time to process all that has happened today. First, I am going to put you in pairs and have you share your reactions to today's session. Then, we'll all meet and close out the session. Andrea, you and Connie pair up. Diane, you and Crystal; and Marti, you and Betty Jo. Get with your partner and talk about your feelings from today.

Summarizing

Most educational and task groups lend themselves to summarization. Often the leader does the summarizing. Some leaders appoint a person at the beginning of each session to be the person who will summarize. This person pays careful attention or even takes notes. During the summary, the leader usually asks for additional comments or reactions. Summarization during the closing phase can be used in some treatment groups, as in the following example.

Example: Summarizing

Leader: I want to summarize our discussion. We talked about the three Rs of anger control. Instead of React, Retreat and Rethink, we discussed how each of you should try to Retreat, Rethink, and then Respond. We talked about various ways of retreating. Anyone recall what we said?

Riley: Get away from the situation

Louie: Count to ten or even twenty.

Jeff: Take yourself away in your mind to a peaceful place.

Leader: That's good. We also talked about how to rethink the situation; that is, to identify the self-talk and dispute it. We learned about looking for "I can't stand it" and "This is awful" types of self-talk. How did we say to change these sentences?

Louie: Something like, "I don't like it, but I can stand it."

Closing after a Tense Session

During some town meeting groups or unit groups, members can get very heated and tempers can flare. When this occurs, the leader should plan a closing that brings people back together as best as possible. For sure, the leader will not want to allow memebers to attack each other during the closing phase.

Example One: Closing after a Tense Session

Leader: We are going to have to stop in a few minutes because it is almost time to catch the bus to go to the AA meeting. I want us to try to bring things to a close. During this time, I don't want people bringing up new things, and I don't want people attacking each other. Everybody understand? (*Members nod.*) I want to summarize the discussion about the television room and what was agreed upon.

Shane: I still don't think it is fair that they get to watch those stupid shows when I want to watch the news!

Leader: Shane, we are going to keep the same policy for one more week while all of us look at other options. This is the best solution we could come up with for now. Also, I am going to check on a second television that we may be able to put in the smoking room.

Shane: But . . .

Leader: Shane, we're closing now—not discussing. What were the specific points that were agreed upon?

For sessions when members have been angry at one another and have had some time to cool off, the leader can try to patch things up a bit during the closing.

Example Two: Closing after a Tense Session

Leader: Things got heated here, especially between Jessica and Robin. I want to spend an extra few minutes as we close to see if the two of you can see each other's viewpoint now that you have had some time to think. (*With a cautious, careful voice*) Do either of you feel like you can let go of some the anger you expressed earlier?

Jessica: (*In an angry voice*) I can't stand it that . . .

Leader: (*In a calm voice*) Jessica, we're trying now to wind down. Do you want to take a stab at patching things up a bit?

Jessica: Oh, all right. If she wants to.

Leader: Good. How about you, Robin?

Feedback to Others

In some treatment groups, an exercise that we call "My Wish for You" can be used to encourage people to try different things. This is effective when some members have worked on some personal issues at a deep emotional level.

Example : Feedback to Others

Leader: We'll be stopping in about five minutes. I'd like us to share what stood out today. (*With a soft, kind voice*) Also, if you have a wish for another member, please share it. Lots of you have worked on some heavy things today. I think this was a particularly good session.

Sharon: I am so glad I shared what I did. I have always been so ashamed. Thanks. And Heidi, my wish for you is that you forgive yourself. That was not your fault.

Tasha: I didn't say much, but I sure did lots of thinking. This was so helpful. Thanks, Sharon, for sharing, and my wish is for Jody. Jody, I hope you see that your life really isn't over and that prison does not have to be hell.

Future Sessions and Evaluation

In some groups, during some part of the closing, the leader has members discuss what they would like for the next session. This helps the leader and members plan for the next meeting. Also, periodically, during the closing phase, the leader can choose to spend extra time to evaluate how the group is going. Members can share what they like and do not like about the meetings and also can bring up changes that they would like to see. Leaders should only do this if they plan to consider the suggestions. Too often, leaders seek feedback but then do not change anything about the group. This leads to resentment on the part of the members.

The Closing Stage

The closing stage refers to the time period that the leader uses to end a series of group sessions. This is usually the last session or part of the last session, although in some cases a leader may take more than one session to end a group, especially if it has been meeting for a number of months. During the closing stage, the leader should focus on reviewing the major points of the group and bringing the group to a close by making sure that loose ends are tied up and that members are feeling reasonably comfortable about the group ending. Also, for most groups, discussion should take place about how to put to use what has happened in the group.

Example: The Closing Stage

Leader: This is our last session and I want to spend some time wrapping up this experience and hearing what you have gained and how you plan to use what you have learned. I want you to take a few minutes and reflect on the entire twenty weeks. We started with lots of information and education about drugs and alcohol, and then moved more into personal sharing about your past. We also talked about some counseling theories that can help you. (*After a brief pause*) On a sheet of paper, I'd like you to list at least five things that you learned and at least three things you are doing or going to do differently. One other thing I'd like you to do is to list the one activity or one thing we did in group that stood out to you the most. I am going to give you five minutes or so to do this; then, we'll spend the rest of the session hearing your comments and talking about how you can build on what you learned here. Again: five things you learned, three things you are doing or going to do differently, and also the one activity that we did that stood out to you.

The closing stage of most correctional groups is not a major deal, but the leader should be sensitive to the fact that there may be times when a group becomes very meaningful to the members. In such groups, the offenders have enjoyed the sharing and closeness, and the ending of the group creates feelings of loss and fear. In cases like this, the leader will want to plan time during the closing to deal with the emotions of the members. In many prison groups, members come and go all the time. For these groups, there is no closing stage, just a closing phase at the end of each session.

Concluding Comments

The closing phase is an esssential part of any group. It is important to allow enough time for closing and to make sure the closing is meaningful. Usually, the closing phase is not more than ten minutes unless it has been a very intense session. Different types of closing activities, including rounds, dyads, or writing, can be used, depending on the type of group. The closing stage is usually the last session of the group and that is the time when the entire group experience is reviewed and discussed along with how members will use what they have learned.

Afterword

We hope this book has served as a very positive introduction to group counseling and that you feel that you have what you need to get started as a group leader. There is much more to learn about group leading, especially with different populations within the correctional system. However, the information in this book should serve as a solid foundation on which you can build. We hope that you feel you know how to plan a group: how to start it and how to end it, and also that you have many ideas of what to do in the middle phase. The key to success as a leader is integrating the knowledge from this book with practical experience either in classes, at your field placement, or at your place of employment. Practice is the best way to learn to lead groups. We hope that this book has given you enough information and ideas so that you will enjoy the experience of becoming a good group leader. We can be reached at *edjacobs@impactherapy.com.* We sincerely welcome your comments, feedback, and any suggestions on how the book can be improved.

References

Adams, L. 1974. Use of TA with Adult Male Prison Inmates. *Transactional Analysis Journal*. 4: 18-19.

Alexander, R. and G. Pratsinak. 2002. *Arresting Addictions: Drug Education and Relapse Prevention in Corrections*. Lanham, Maryland: American Correctional Association.

Amen, D. G. 1998. *Change Your Brain, Change Your Life: The Breakthrough Program For Conquering Anxiety, Depression, Obsessiveness, Anger, and Impulsiveness*. New York: Random House.

Arbuthnot, J. 1984. Moral Reasoning Development Programs in Prisons: Cognitive-Developmental and Critical Reasoning Approaches. *Journal of Moral Education*. 13(2): 112-123.

Beck, A. T. and M. Weishaar. 1995. Cognitive Therapy. In R. Corsini and D. Wedding, eds. *Current Psychotherapies*, 5th ed. Itasca, Illinois: F. E. Peacock. pp. 229-261.

Blinn, Cynthia. 1997. *Maternal Ties: A Selection of Programs for Female Offenders.* Lanham, Maryland: American Correctional Association.

Boesky, Lisa. 2002. *Juvenile Offenders with Mental Health Disorders: Who Are They? And What Do We Do with Them?* Lanham, Maryland: American Correctional Association.

Braly, M. 1976. *False Starts*. Boston: Little Brown.

Carp, S. and L. Schade. 1992. Tailoring Facility Programming to Suit Female Offenders Needs. *Corrections Today*. 54(6): 152-159.

Clement, M. 1993. Parenting in Prisons: A National Survey of Programs for Incarcerated Women. *Journal of Offender Rehabilitation.* 19: 89-100.

Cohen, B. and I. Sordo. 1984. Using Reality Therapy with Adult Offenders. *Journal of Offender Counseling, Services, and Rehabilitation*. 8: 25-39.

Corey, G. 2000. *The Theory and Practice of Group Counseling,* 5th ed. Pacific Grove, California: Brooks/Cole.

Corey, G. and M. S. Corey. 2002. *Groups: Process and Practice*, 6th ed. Pacific Grove, California: Brooks/Cole.

Cornelius, G. 2001. *The Art of the Con: Avoiding Offender Manipulation*. Lanham, Maryland: American Correctional Association.

Crawford, J. 1988. *Tabulation of a Nationwide Survey of State Correctional Facilities for Adult and Juvenile Female Offenders*. College Park, Maryland: American Correctional Association.

Cullen, M. 1992. *Cage Your Rage*. Lanham, Maryland: American Correctional Association.

Cullen, M. and S. Piekarski. 2002. *TRY: Treatment Readiness for You: A Workbook for Abusers in Relationships*. Lanham, Maryland: American Correctional Association.

DeLucia-Waack, J. L. 1996. Multiculturalism Is Inherent in All Group Work. *Journal for Specialists in Group Work*. 21(4): 218-223.

Donigian, J. and D. Hulse-Killacky. 1999. *Critical Incidents in Group Therapy*, 2nd ed. Pacific Grove, California: Brooks/Cole.

Elliot, W. and V. Verdeyen. 2003. *Game Over: Strategies for Redirecting Inmate Deception*. Lanham, Maryland: American Correctional Association.

Ellis, A. and W. Dryden. 1997. *The Practice of Rational Emotive Behavior Therapy*, rev. ed. Secaucus, New Jersey: Lyle Stuart.

Faith, K. 1993. *Unruly Women: The Politics of Confinement and Resistance*. Vancouver: Press Gang.

Forester-Miller, H. and J. A. Kottle. 1997. *Issues and Challenges for Group Practitioners*. Denver: Love.

Gaudin, J. and D. Kurtz. 1985. Parenting Skills Training for Child Abusers. *Journal of Group Psychotherapy, Psychodrama, and Sociometry*. 31: 35-54.

Gendreau, P. 1996. Offender Rehabilitation: What We Know and What Needs to Be Done. *Criminal Justice and Behavior*. 23: 144-161.

Gibbs, J., K. Arnold, H. Ahlborn, and F. Cheesman. 1984. Facilitation of Sociomoral Reasoning in Delinquents. *Journal of Consulting and Clinical Psychology*. 52(1): 37-45.

Gladding, S. T. 1992. *Counseling as an Art: The Creative Arts in Counseling*. Alexandria, Virginia: American Counseling Association.

———. 2003. *Group Work: A Counseling Specialty*, 4th ed. New York: Merrill.

Glasser, W. 1965. *Reality Therapy: A New Approach to Psychiatry*. New York: Harper and Row.

———. 1998. *Choice Theory: A New Psychology of Personal Freedom*. New York: HarperCollins.

Glick, B. and W. Sturgeon. 2002. *Recess Is Over: A Handbook for Managing Youthful Offenders in Adult Systems*. Lanham, Maryland: American Correctional Association.

Goldstein, A. and B. Glick. 1987. *Aggression Replacement Training*. Champaign, Illinois: Research Press.

Haskell, M. 1960. Group Psychotherapy and Psychodrama in Prison. *Group Psychotherapy*. 13: 22-33.

Heffernan, R. 1972. *The Square, the Cool, and the Life*. New York: John Wiley.

Hulse-Killacky, D., J. Killacky, and J. Donigian. 2001. *Making Task Groups Work in Your World*. Upper Saddle River, New Jersey: Merrill Prentice Hall.

Jackson, D. and L. Myers. 2002. *Reality Therapy and Choice Theory: Managing Behavior Today, Developing Skills for Tomorrow*. Lanham, Maryland: American Correctional Association.

Jackson, L. 1998. *Gangbusters: Strategies for Prevention and Intervention*. Lanham, Maryland: American Correctional Association.

Jacobs, E. 1992. *Creative Counseling Techniques: An Illustrated Guide*. Odessa, Florida: Psychological Assessment Resources.

———. 1994. *Impact Therapy*. Odessa, Florida: Psychological Assessment Resources.

Jacobs, E., R. Masson, and R. Harvill. 2002. *Group Counseling: Strategies and Skills*, 4th ed. Pacific Grove, California: Brooks/Cole.

Jesness, C. 1975. Comparative Effectiveness of Behavior Modification and Transactional Programs for Delinquents. *Journal of Consulting and Clinical Psychology*. 43: 759-799.

Johnson, D. W. and F. P. Johnson. 2000. *Joining Together*, 7th ed. Boston: Allyn and Bacon.

Kassebaum, G. W., D. A. Ward, and D. M. Wilner. 1971. *Prison Treatment and Parole Survival: An Empirical Assessment*. New York: John Wiley and Sons.

Kauffman, K. 2001. Mothers in Prison. *Corrections Today*. 63(1): 62-66.

Kees, N. and E. Jacobs. 1990. Conducting More Effective Groups: How to Select and Process Group Exercises. *Journal for Specialists in Group Work*. 15(1): 21–30.

Kottler, J. A. 1994. *Advanced Group Leadership*. Pacific Grove, California: Brooks/Cole.

Latessa, E., ed. 1999. *Strategic Solutions: The International Community Corrections Association Examines Substance Abuse—What Works*. Lanham, Maryland: International Community Corrections Association and American Correctional Association.

Lombardo, V. and R. Smith. 1996. Rational Emotive Therapy: A Model Program for Female Offenders. *Corrections Today*. 10: 92-95.

Marshall, W. 1996. Assessment, Treatment, and Theorizing about Sex Offenders. *Criminal Justice and Behavior*. 23: 162-199.

Masters, R. 1994. *Counseling and Criminal Justice Offenders*. Thousand Oaks, California: Sage.

Maultsby, M. C. 1984. *Rational Behavior Therapy*. Englewood Cliffs, New Jersey: Prentice Hall.

Miller, M. 1960. Psychodrama in the Treatment Program of a Juvenile Court. *Journal of Criminal Law, Criminology, and Police Science*. 50: 453-459.

Moreno, J. 1964. *Psychodrama: Volume 1,* rev. ed. New York: Beacon Press.

Morton, J. B. and D. M. Williams. 1998. Mother/Child Bonding. *Corrections Today*. 60(7): 98-105.

Nicholson, R. 1970. Transactional Analysis. *Federal Probation*. 34: 29-38.

Owen, B. 1998. *In the Mix: Struggle and Survival in a Women's Prison*. New York: State University of New York Press.

Parks, G. A. and G. A. Marlatt. 1999. *Keep "What Works" Working: Cognitive-Behavioral Relapse Prevention Therapy with Substance Abusing Offenders*. In E. J. Latessa, ed. *Strategic Solutions: The International Community Corrections Association Examines Substance Abuse—What Works*. Lanham, Maryland: International Community Corrections Association and American Correctional Association.

Pollock, J. 1998. *Counseling Women in Prison*. Thousand Oaks, California: Sage.

Posthuma, B. W. 1999. *Small Groups in Therapy Settings: Process and Leadership,* 3rd ed. Boston: Allyn and Bacon.

Prettyman, E. B. 1981. The Indeterminate Sentence and the Right to Treatment. In D. Fogel and J. Hudson, eds. *Justice as Fairness: Perspectives on the Justice Model*. Cincinnati, Ohio: Anderson Publishing Co.

Read, E. 1996. *Partners in Change: The 12 Step Referral Handbook for Probation, Parole and Community Corrections*. Lanham, Maryland: American Correctional Association.

Ross, R., E. Fabiano, and C. Ewles. 1988. Reasoning and Rehabilitation. *International Journal of Offender Therapy and Comparative Criminology.* 32(1): 29-35.

Rottman, E. 1990. *Beyond Punishment.* New York: Greenwood Press.

Samenow, S. 1984. *Inside the Criminal Mind.* New York: Time Books.

Schrumski, T., C. Feldman, D. Harvey, and M. Holiman. 1984. A Comparative Evaluation of Group Treatments in an Adult Correctional Facility. *Journal of Group Psychotherapy, Psychodrama, and Sociometry.* 36: 133-147.

Silverman, I. J. and M. Vega. 1996. *Corrections: A Comprehensive View.* New York: West Publishing Co.

Smith A. B. and L. Berlin. 1988. *Treating the Criminal Offender.* New York: Plenum Press.

Snell, T. 1994. *Women in Prison: Survey of State Prison Inmates, 1991.* U.S. Department of Justice, Bureau of Justice Statistics Special Report. Washington, D.C.: Government Printing Office.

Stojkovic, S. and R. Lovell. 1997. *Corrections: An Introduction,* 2nd ed. Cincinnati, Ohio: Anderson Publishing Company.

Twerski, A. J. 1997. *Addictive Thinking,* 2nd ed. Center City, Minnesota: Hazelden.

Van Voorhis, P., M. Braswell, and D. Lester. 2000. *Correctional Counseling and Rehabilitation,* 4th ed. Cincinnati, Ohio: Anderson Publishing Company.

Verdeyen, V. 1999. Changing the Criminal Mind. *Corrections Today.* 61(1): 52-54.

Vernon, A. 1995. *Thinking, Feeling, Behaving: An Emotional Education Curriculum for Adolescents/Grades 7-12.* Champaign, Illinois: Research Press.

Walen, S., R. DiGiuseppe, and W. Dryden. 1992. *A Practitioner's Guide to Rational Emotive Therapy.* New York: Oxford University Press.

Walsh, A. 2001. *Correctional Assessment, Casework, and Counseling,* 3rd ed. Lanham, Maryland: American Correctional Association.

Ward, D. and G. Kassebaum. 1965. *Women's Prison: Sex and Social Structure.* Hawthorne, New York: Adeline.

Welo, B. 2001. *Tough Customers: Counseling Unwilling Clients.* Lanham, Maryland: American Correctional Association.

Wojda, R. G. and J. Rowse. 1997. *Women Behind Bars.* Lanham, Maryland: American Correctional Association.

Wubbolding, R. 2000. *Reality Therapy for the 21st Century.* New York: Brunner/Mazel.

Yalom, I. 1995. *The Theory and Practice of Group Psychotherapy,* 4th ed. New York: Basic Books.

Index

A

B

C

D

E

F

G

H

I

J

K

L

M

N

O

P

Q

R

S

T

U

V

W

Y

About the Authors

Ed Jacobs, Ph.D., has taught group counseling for thirty years at West Virginia University, where he currently is the coordinator of the masters program in counseling. His book, *Group Counseling: Strategies and Skills*, is in its fourth edition and is used throughout the United States to train counselors and students. Because of his outstanding contributions to the field of group counseling, Dr. Jacobs is one of few to be selected as a Fellow in the Association for Specialists in Group Work, a division of the American Counseling Association. He received his bachelor of arts degree and his master of arts degree in psychology from the University of Texas at Austin. He received his Ph.D. in counselor education from Florida State University. Dr. Jacobs conducts numerous workshops on group counseling each year and has served as a trainer on many occasions for the Federal

Bureau of Prisons. He currently is serving as a consultant and trainer for both juvenile and adult corrections in West Virginia and hopes to establish a model group program in the state correctional system. Please send questions, comments, or feedback about this book to:
edjacobs@impacttherapy.com.

Nina Spadaro, Ed.D., was a staff psychologist for ten years for the Federal Bureau of Prisons, where she led mandatory Drug Abuse Prevention (DAP) groups, orientation and prerelease groups. After developing several successful voluntary psycho-educational counseling groups, she was asked to develop, coordinate, and implement an interdisciplinary therapeutic intensive program, which was centered around concepts of wellness. Dr. Spadaro also developed and maintained the Family Enrichment Program for the Federal Correctional Institution (FCI) Morgantown, West Virginia, which included leading both educational and task groups for inmates and their families. In 1992, she was awarded the Sustained Superior Performance Award in recognition of the outstanding training sessions she provided FCI Morgantown staff. She earned her bachelor of science degree in psychology from Fordham University, and her master's degree in rehabilitation counseling, and her doctorate of education in counseling from West Virginia University. Currently, she is in private practice and teaches group counseling at the graduate level for West Virginia University. She also provides group training workshops for those who work with at-risk youth in community programs and group homes.